Founder's Pocket Guide: Raising An

1x1MEDIA

Simple, quick answers, all in one place.

By

Stephen R. Poland

1x1 Media
Asheville, North Carolina
United States

Care has been taken to verify the accuracy of information in this book. However, the authors and publisher cannot accept responsibility for consequences from application of the information in this book, and makes no warranty, expressed or implied, with respect to its content.

Trademarks: Some of the product names and company names included in this book have been used for identification purposes only and may be trademarks or registered trade names of their respective manufacturers and sellers. The author and publisher disclaim any affiliation, association, or connection with, or sponsorship or endorsement by, such owners.

ISBN 978-1-938162-10-7

©2017 by 1x1 Media, LLC

email: info@1x1media.com

website : www.1x1media.com

Table of Contents

Founder's Pocket Guide:
Raising Angel Capital

"It's hard to do a really good job on anything you don't think about in the shower."

- Paul Graham, YCombinator co-founder

What the Founder's Pocket Guide Series Delivers

We developed the *Founder's Pocket Guide* series to provide quick answers to common questions encountered by entrepreneurs. Consider the following dilemmas:

> "I sort of know **what startup equity is**, but really don't understand the details, and I have an investor interested in my company. Where do I start?"

> "My co-founder said we need to **build a cap table to track our equity ownership**—how do we get started?"

> "My co-founders and I need to determine **how to divide the ownership** of our startup, but how can we be certain we get it right?"

> "I've heard that **convertible debt is a good funding structure for early-stage startups**. What is convertible debt and how do I approach potential investors with a funding pitch?"

The *Founder's Pocket Guide* series addresses each of the topics in a concise and easy to reference format.

Look for these current titles at www.1x1media.com:

- *Founder's Pocket Guide: Founder Equity Splits*
- *Founder's Pocket Guide: Startup Valuation*
- *Founder's Pocket Guide: Term Sheets*
- *Founder's Pocket Guide: Startup Valuation*
- *Founder's Pocket Guide: Friends & Family Funding*
- *Founder's pocket Guide: Comvertible Debt*

Disclaimers

The content in this guide is not intended as legal, financial, or tax advice and cannot be relied upon for any purpose without the services of a qualified professional. With that disclaimer in mind, here's our position on how to best use the guidance provided in this work.

Great entrepreneurs use all the resources available to them, making the best decisions they can to mitigate risk and yet move ahead with the most important tasks in their roadmaps. This process includes consulting lawyers, CPAs, and other professionals with deep domain knowledge when necessary.

Great entrepreneurs also balance a strong do-it-yourself drive with the understanding that the whole team creates great innovations and succeeds in bringing great products to the world. Along those lines, here's a simple plan for the scrappy early-stage founder who can't afford to hire a startup lawyer or CPA to handle all of the tasks needed to close a funding deal or form the startup:

1. **Educate yourself on what's needed.** Learn about startup equity structures and issues, legal agreements, financing structures, and other company formation best practices, and then;

2. **Get your lawyer involved**. Once you thoroughly understand the moving parts and have completed some of the work to the best of your ability, pay your startup-experienced lawyer or other professional to advise you and finalize the legal contracts.

With this self-educating and money-saving sequence in mind, let's dig in to this *Founder's Pocket Guide*.

In This Pocket Guide

This guide provides a detailed review of the complete angel funding process, as well as an introduction to many key concepts entrepreneurs need to know. For easy navigation, the book includes many headings and bold-faced key points. This helps you skip forward, scan for what you need, and continue to build your startup knowledge.

Overall, this *Founder's Pocket Guide* addresses these five key areas:

- Understanding what angel investing is, and what motivates angel investors
- Deciphering what angels look for in startups
- Walking through the angel funding process
- Making your startup investor ready
- Building your startup funding process knowledge

Drilling down, the book answers questions such as:

- What stage does my startup need to be at to be interesting to angel investors?
- How much equity should I give up to investors?
- How much money can I realistically raise from angels?
- When should my team start to raise money?
- Is my startup right for angel investors?
- How much can my startup legally raise?
- What do terms such as dilution, convertible debt, and cap table mean?
- What is the difference between preferred shares and common shares?
- What is a term sheet, and how does it impact an investment?

To kick things off, let's get an understanding of angel investors, what industry segments they invest in, and what drives their investment decisions.

1

Understanding Angel Investors

Angels or angel investors are high net worth individuals that invest in startups and early stage ventures, either independently, or in organized angel groups (also called angel investor groups). The following sections dig into several angel investor characteristics, helping startup founders better prepare for the fundraising process.

Angels Have Made Their Wealth in Many Ways

The source of an investor's wealth might not seem relevant to an entrepreneur seeking capital. Money is money, right? In reality, an angel's background and the source of his or her funds speaks volumes about the types of startups they will understand and how they are likely to interact with the founders. Ideal angels for your startup come from, or understand, your kind of startup. For example, if you are a Web startup, then angels that have started successful Web companies are good matches. Be sure to consider how prospective angels got to where they are. Examples include:

- **Successful entrepreneurs** have sold their company and have money to invest, and want to assist other entrepreneurs.

- **Corporate executives** have high paying positions and want to invest in new ideas and technology. They are often able to connect with investment opportunities within their industry.

11

- **Highly paid professionals**, including doctors, lawyers, dentists, and others, often have excess cash and are motivated by a desire for high investment returns.

- **Individuals from wealthy families** have legacy money earned from current and past generations, so they establish "family offices" to manage foundations and fund startup investments.

Angels Invest in Growth Segments

Angels invest in segments and industries that are experiencing high growth. Startups in Internet, healthcare, and mobile segments received 69% of the angel group investment deals in 2012. Figure 1 shows the breakdown of angel group investing, as reported in the 2012 Halo Report

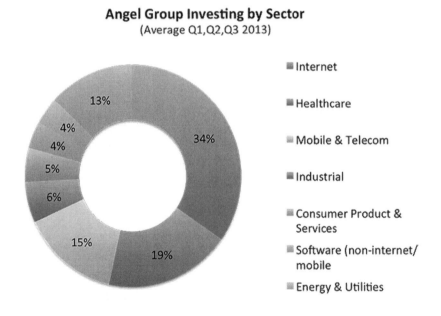

Figure 1. Angel group investing by sector.

Why Angels Invest

Wealthy people choose to get involved in angel investing for many reasons. From the founder's perspective, gaining some insight to an investor's motivation can help create better alignment between the startup and the investor. Example investor motivations include:

- **High Financial Returns.** Angels hope to get returns 10% to 15% higher than other investing options. For example, returns on the S&P stock index have averaged 11% annually, so angels hope for 20-25% returns on the money they invest in your startup.

- **Economic Development.** Angels seek to help young companies grow in their local area, creating a supportive environment for startups and entrepreneurs, as well as more established and growing small to midsize businesses.

- **Giving Back.** Angels have successfully sold their startup and want to help other entrepreneurs build their companies. Sometimes called guardian angels, successful (and recently wealthy) entrepreneurs make ideal funding partners for startups.

- **Changing the World.** Some investors are highly motivated to make the world a better place. Referred to as impact investors, these individuals and groups seek startups that will impact large numbers of disadvantaged populations or segments of our economy. Impact investors target the clean water, green energy, and education segments, among others.

- **Excitement.** Angels like being a part of the high energy, dynamic startup culture. Getting involved with startups is a good way to see new technology and trends.

Independent Angels

Some angels prefer to invest by themselves, not as part of a group. These individuals offer entrepreneurs some advantages in fundraising, including:

- They can sometimes make deals quickly, compared with organized angel groups.

- They can be "first money in" for many startups, which helps validate the startup for later investors.

- They are often motivated to invest as a vote of support for the entrepreneur, more than investing in the idea, technology, or company.

- They can serve as an experienced mentor, helping guide inexperienced founders through the startup process.

Networking and personal referrals are the best way to find independent angels.

Organized Angel Groups

Many investors prefer to join organized angel groups. The group model offers the angels several benefits:

- Members of the group can share the workload of screening and vetting startups.

- With many different levels of investing experience likely to be represented in the group, members new to angel investing can learn from seasoned angels.

- By establishing processes for evaluating startups, the group takes the guesswork out of how to build its investment portfolio.

- To join an angel group, an investor usually buys in with a contribution of $25,000 or so, adding to the pool of funds the group has to invest.

- An angel group typically meets on a regular schedule, making sure potential new investments are evaluated in a timely fashion.

- An angel group likely has pre-prepared legal documents, eliminating the need to reinvent the wheel for every deal.

- Angel groups are less likely to want to be involved day by day in your startup's business activities, in contrast to some independent angels who might want very active participation, such as arranging customer meetings, attending industry events, assisting with short term strategy planning, and so on.

Most angel groups develop specific criteria that determine the nature and scope of the group's investments. For example, an angel group might:

- Focus on a specific niche such as biotech or Web and Internet technology, based on the expertise of the group members.

- Occasionally limit investment amounts in some way, for example no more than 10% of the total fund into any one startup.

- Set a top-end limit on the startup's valuation, such as only considering startups that have pre-money valuations of $2 million or less.

- Avoid being the first investor, saying they do not want to be the "first money in." Many angel groups would like to see other investors take on some of the early risk in the venture. Independent angels can help pave the way for organized angel groups in this way.

- Seek startups with well established intellectual property (IP), including patented or patentable products.

Benefits of Working with Organized Angels

While working with an independent angel might seem like the simplest way to go for a founder, organized angel groups offer startups many advantages, such as:

- **Higher Investment Amounts.** Angel groups have pooled their member's money and tend to invest in many deals. More deals equates to an increased likelihood of success. All of this means the angel group tend to have larger pools of money to invest, and the confidence of past successful exits. These pluses enable groups to invest a larger amount in each deal. Larger groups in areas such as New York or Seattle might invest as much as $500,000 in a single startup. [2013 Halo report]

- **Accredited.** The group members meet the Securities and Exchange Commission (SEC) accredited investor requirements, and in theory, have the money to lose if their investments go bad.

- **Sophisticated.** They are sophisticated in the eyes of the SEC, meaning they are experienced in business matters and can assess the risks of an investment.

- **Legally Clean.** Organized angels make sure their investments meet the requirements of the SEC securities registration exemptions, and experienced lawyers hired by the group manage all legal paperwork.

- **Risk Tolerant.** Angel group members understand the risks of startup investing and are unlikely to suffer personally or sue if they lose their money on your venture. (Less sophisticated investors and families might not understand the risks of committing their life savings to a startup investment and can experience serious financial hardship if the investment doesn't pay off.)

Downsides of Working with Organized Angel Groups

There are some downsides of working with angel groups, including:

- **10 Angels, 10 Opinions.** One vocal angel in the room can negatively influence the entire group, causing them to pass on an investment. Having a champion angel on your side can be an antidote to this problem.

- **Slow Process.** Many meetings and due diligence conducted by a group does not inherently promote speedy decision making.

- **Limited Availability.** Groups can be dealing with many startups at one time, so getting on the agenda for a meeting can be challenging and require persistence.

- **Expectation of Process Knowledge.** When entrepreneurs pitch to angel groups, there is an unspoken expectation that the entrepreneur understands the "game" of startup fundraising (the mission of this guide). The angels expect that the entrepreneur knows the terminology and has a basic understanding of topics such as valuation, equity, and investment deal structures. You don't have to be an expert in every detail—advisors and lawyers can help guide you through the process—but a good understanding of these areas should be part of every founder's homework.

- **Reputation to Protect.** Angel groups want to build a track record of picking great startups, so groups tend to be very selective in committing investment dollars to startups.

Angels vs. VCs: It's Their Money

Whether organized or independent, angels are investing their own money. Venture capitalists (VCs) and private equity groups are investing other people's money (OPM), from sources such as private foundations, pension plans, university capital funds, and so on. This is one of the major differences between angels and VCs.

As a result, VCs often can and will exert much more control over a startup, such as installing an experienced CEO and requiring a board of directors (BOD) seat. That being said, because VCs have access to much larger pools of money, the scale and terms of a VC deal can differ greatly from an angel deal. The following examples highlight the key differences between an angel level deal and a VC scale deal.

Typical Independent or Group Angel Investment Deal

- $150,000 to $1 million invested (total round).
- Valuation of $1 to $3 million maximum. (See the section titled "Valuation Methods" for details on startup valuations.)
- Angel equity of 20% to 40%
- Expect to exit the investment in 5 to 7 years
- Mix of active vs. passive participation in the startup company
- BOD seat or some level of oversight
- Wants to split investment with other angels or angel groups

Typical VC Investment Deal

- $500,000 to $5 million or more (total round 1).
- Valuation in the $2 to $15 million range.
- VC Equity 17-35% with preferred rights. (See the section titled "Preferred Shares vs. Common Shares" for more details.)
- Expect to exit the investment in 3 to 7 years.
- Active participation in management of the startup company.
- Decision making oversight control (can fire founders); drive the startup for growth and exit.
- Multiple VCs tend to co-invest in a startup, spreading the risk, and increasing the investment amount.

Deal Syndication and Sidecars

Many angel groups co-invest with other groups. If your startup can win over one angel group, you might be able to syndicate a deal with other angel groups. Your local group vets your startup, performs due diligence, and leads the way with an investment, and then encourages sister/affiliated angel groups to invest as well.

Once an angel group decides to invest a portion of the group's fund in a startup, individuals within the angel group might want more of the action. In this case, they can choose to invest personal money in the startup, under the same deal terms negotiated with the group. These additional investments are called sidecars or add-ons.

Accredited Investor Status

To join an angel group or invest as an independent angel, you must meet the SEC's accredited investor criteria. The SEC defines an accredited investor (under Rule 501 of Reg D: http://www.sec.gov/answers/regd.htm) as:

- a natural person who has individual net worth, or joint net worth with the person's spouse, that exceeds $1 million, excluding the value of the primary residence of such person, or;

- a natural person with income exceeding $200,000 in each of the two most recent years or joint income with a spouse exceeding $300,000 for those years and a reasonable expectation of the same income level in the current year

The SEC accredited investor criteria is designed to help protect both investors and companies seeking investors. Investors that meet the wealth hurdles have the money to lose (in theory), and entrepreneurs raising money for their startup have some assurance that the investors have money to put at risk. See section "SEC Rules of Startup Funding" for more details about the SEC rules for raising money for your venture.

Finding Angel Investors

Finding angel investors has become a much easier task with the help of the Internet. The following overview lists a few of the top online resources, as well as giving some pointers to offline ways to connect with investors.

The Angel Capital Association. This nonprofit professional and trade association is dedicated to advancing angel investing by supporting both angel investors and entrepreneurs. The association has over 200 member angel groups, with more than 10,000 individual investor members. Founders can locate angel groups in their region via the "Links to Member Groups" section of the site (www.angelcapitalassociation.org).

Online Funding Sites. Several websites endeavor to create ecosystems to connect entrepreneurs and angel investors. One example, Gust.com, provides an online platform for founders to submit details about their startup to an online community of angel investors. Once the startup has granted access to an interested angel group, the investors can review business plans, financial forecasts, and video pitches uploaded by the founders. From the angel perspective, angels use the platform to discuss and rate the startups they are interested in. Once the initial connection has been made via the Gust website, investors can arrange in-person meeting with the entrepreneurs, arrange a pitch meeting, and hopefully move on to deeper due diligence of the startup.

Public Funding. AngelList (angel.co) is another online effort designed to connect promising startups with investors. Using the AngelList platform, the startup creates a profile and lets the general public see the startup information. Investors also sign up with the platform, provide verification of accredited status, and then review the profiles of startups listed on the site. If an investor wants to contact a startup about investing, the investor can message the startup and begin the discussion.

In SEC lingo, announcing to the world (aka the Internet) that you are raising funding is called "general solicitation" and was historically not allowed for startups. As of September 2013, startups can use general solicitation to find investors to help fund their startup. In a general solicitation situation, investors **must be accredited**, with strict guidelines for evaluating accredited status. Founders must request documentation such as tax returns or written confirmation from certified professionals such as the investor's CPA or lawyer. AngelList helps with this process by requiring investors to provide this kind of verification, but it is still incumbent on the entrepreneur to take whatever steps are needed to be sure of any investor's status.

 Avoiding TMI

If you choose to explore the public funding via site like AngelList, be sure the information you provide in your online profile does not include financial projections or other forward looking speculations. While this seems counterintuitive to everything you've been taught about selling your startup to investors (including what you'll read in this book), steer clear of statements like "We're going to make millions, and here's how." Legally, these kinds of statements combined with raising money from people you don't really know make a volatile recipe that can become a basis for lawsuits if the stated results do not materialize. Be sure to stick to facts, not forecasts, in the descriptive information you post. For example, compare two example statements from the AngelList site. Fact: "Our users grew 20% last month." Forecast: "We're going to grow 20% a month."

Other Online Startup Resources. Numerous websites and blogs cover startups and angel funding. Sites such as CrunchBase (www. crunchbase.com) and Hacker News (news.ycombinator.com) provide inspiring and detailed data about funding rounds and startup exits, as well as blog posts centered on the successes and woes of startup life. Sorting though all of the startup blogs and angel investment sites can consume a lot of time, so be sure to stay focused on topics impacting *your* startup and goals.

Going Local. Most moderately sized cities (over 150,000) have organized angel groups. Locating angel groups in your local area is as easy as searching online for your city name and "angel investor". Sort through the inevitable search engine clutter, and locate the organized angel groups operating your area. You can cold call the group organizer, but a warm introduction to the group is a more effective way to begin the relationship. To arrange a warm introduction, seek out local economic support organizations such as business incubators, nonprofit small business support groups like SCORE (formerly Service Core of Retired Executives), or other business service providers such as CPAs or patent attorneys. The support organizations in particular often have established connections to any local angel group and can help make a warm introduction.

Other Entrepreneurs. Your fellow entrepreneurs can be one of the best sources to local angel investors. Attend local events and meet ups centered on entrepreneurship, and network with the founders you meet. Most savvy startup founders know that sharing their connections, angels included, make the overall entrepreneurial community stronger, so they are happy to share their connections, experiences, and knowledge.

Incubators, Accelerators, and University Startup Programs. These organizations are created with the express purpose of helping entrepreneurs. If your area has one of these organizations, get in touch, tell the contact person your story, and see where the connections can lead. Angel groups often use incubators and startup accelerators for deal flow, seeking the higher caliber entrepreneurs typically spawned from programs for developing new businesses.

Chambers of Commerce. While typically focused on supporting existing local small businesses, many Chambers of Commerce now offer support for the startup entrepreneurs in the community. Be sure to check in with your local chamber about opportunities to connect with angel investors.

Investing Close to Home

Location, location, location applies in angel investing as well as real estate. The majority of angels invest close to home, with 81% of angel deals in 2012 made in the home state of the angel. While in other areas of business the digital age makes physical separation a non issue, investors want to be close to their money, check in with entrepreneurs, meet face to face, and experience the excitement (or stress) of the startup process. High concentrations of angels and angel groups are found in major cities such as Boston, New York, Atlanta, Chicago, greater Seattle, and of course the Silicon Valley region.

Exit Expectation: How Investors Get Their Money Back

When you raise angel money, it usually is understood that you are building your startup to be acquired by a larger company or go public, either of which is known as an exit or liquidity event. The investors, founders, employees, and anybody else who holds an equity stake (shares) in the startup divide the proceeds of the exit.

In an acquisition or merger situation, you sell or merge your company with a larger entity. Ownership and control transfers to the acquirer and existing shareholders (the angels/VCs and others) are bought out at some multiple of their original share price. This is the most common form of exit for investors.

Angels and other investors hope for the startup to be ready for exit within three to five years. The price paid for startups by the acquiring company can vary widely, but it is usually expressed as a **multiple of the startup's annual revenue or profit**. Exit multiples range from lows of one times revenue (referred to as 1X) to highs of 5X or more. The amount of the exit proceeds received by angel investors depends on a number of factors, such as the percentage of shares owned, special share preferences, and the rights of other investors such as VCs. Angels take large amounts of risk by investing at the early stages of a startup, and for that risk, they hope to e rewarded if the company has a exit. An investment return of **at least five to ten times** the money put in is considered a win for the angel or angel group.

There are four other possible outcomes from an investment in a startup:

- **IPO.** The startup is taken public (initial public offering), with shares sold by Wall Street investment bankers. IPOs are becoming somewhat more common, but still rare compared to the number of startups that are acquired.

- **Acqui-hire.** A recent phenomenon, in an acqui-hire a larger company acquires the startup for its employees, not for the startup's product or service. .Scarcity of top-notch technical talent sometimes makes it cheaper for a large company to acquire a large batch of skilled employees by buying a smaller startup. This type of exit typically yields a smaller return on investment for investors, as compared to an acquisition motivated by strategic or financial returns.

- **Buyback.** The startup buys back the shares owned by the investors. Buybacks are rare. They are a compromise deal at best, meaning the startup is surviving, but the growth potential that was hoped for is not coming to be. Angels are happy to get out of the deal with something.

- **Complete Loss.** The high risk nature of new and innovative ventures is directly tied to their high failure rate. Books brim with examples of why trying and failing is ultimately the only path to success. Angels and other investors live with this reality and accept the fact that many of their investments will "go to zero." More than one third of angel deals result in a complete loss.

To offset high risk, angels invest in a portfolio of startups, and winning deals must offset losing deals. Some of the startups in the portfolio need to really hit it big to make up for the deals that fall flat or completely implode.

Vetting Prospective Angel Investors

Angel investors can help startups in many ways beyond money. Founders should attempt to find "ideal" angels who add more than money to their relationship with the startup. The ideal angel should be a partner and advocate, not a critic or judge.

Ideal angel traits include:

- **Product and Industry Knowledge.** Investors with experience with your kind of product, such as mobile apps, SaaS (Software as a Service), or other physical consumer products such as electronic devices, specialty foods, clothing and fashion, or sporting and outdoor items can contribute technical expertise that helps improve the offering or overcome obstacles in manufacturing, sourcing, and more.

- **Customer Insider.** Investors may have personal connections with potential customers or industry partners, brining the ability to connect your startup to your market.

- **Technical Expertise.** Some investors are experts and have deep technical knowledge, such as engineering or scientific experience. Others may have hard to find specialty understanding, such as medical device testing and approval processes. Such investors tend to bring credibility to the startup venture, and may contribute specific help with design and processes.

- **Startup Knowledge.** Angels with direct previous experience in the startup process bring additional experience with raising money and building teams. They may also mentor founders on tricky issues encountered when building a company, such as how to fire someone, handle disruptive investors, and so on.

Founders should perform their own due diligence on the angel investors they are courting. Think of it as reverse due diligence. A bad relationship with an investor can be very disruptive to a startup. Doing thorough research about potential investors can save founders many headaches down the road. You can find out more about an angel or angel group considering an investment in your company by speaking with others in your local entrepreneurial community, by asking detailed questions of the angel(s), and so on. No matter the source of the information, key questions to answer cover these areas:

- **Investing Experience.** Has the angel invested in startups before, and if so, what kinds? Inexperienced investors can ask for updates and endless what-if scenarios. Experienced angels limit the workload put on the founders and can lead you to other investors.

- **Startup References.** Check with other startups funded by the investor. Are the founders happy with the relationship? What's good and what's not so good about the relationship?

- **Previous Wins.** Has the angel had successes in your local area? Have other startups exited and rewarded the angel?

- **Values Match.** Is the angel involved and active in your local community? Does the angel's actions and activities outside of investing match your values?

2

What Attributes Do Angels Want in a Startup?

Angel investors look for a number of favorable characteristics in the startups they invest in, including:

- Great teams
- Large target market size
- Disruptive technology or ideas
- Customer traction and retention
- Defensible IP or market position
- High growth potential (three to five years)
- Scalable model

The following sections detail these factors.

Great Teams

Investors look for "A-level" teams, choosing to invest because of the people—the founders, and their team—not because of the technology, product, or idea. Many changes and challenges occur during the early months and years of the startup, and experienced founders can navigate around obstacles and pivot to meet customer needs as understanding of those needs evolves.

Offsetting Lack of Founder Experience

Inexperienced startup teams often have trouble raising angel funding, but customer traction cures everything. If the uptake on your product or service is significant, investors will quickly ignore an inexperienced founding team. Other factors mitigate lack of experience:

- Good process knowledge of startups and funding

- Well-rounded and coachable founders

- Well respected advisors and mentors

- Resourcefulness in achieving startup milestones

Other characteristics of an A-level team might include:

- **Previous Startup Experience.** Founders who have launched other startups or worked as employees in other startups have an advantage in convincing angels to invest. Even if the founders' previous startup experience ended with the startup's failure, experienced investors highly value previous startup experience.

- **Successful Funding Rounds.** Founders who have raised angel funding in previous startups are well liked by angels. They understand the funding process, know the terminology, and tend to present their startup in a concise manner, answering hot button topics ahead of the questions of the angels.

- **Deep Domain Knowledge.** Technical founders who have deep knowledge of their industry and technology add to the perception of a strong team. Many startups are created because the founders work in other companies doing in the trenches technical work, and they "see a better way." They leave their employer and found their own startup.

- **Previous Exit Success.** Founders who have "gone all the way" and have previously led their startup to getting acquired are the rock stars of the startup world. Investors have higher confidence that the founder can repeat prior success and are quick to invest if the other traits of the startup look solid.

- **More Than One Founder.** Investors like startups that have more than one founder. There are too many tasks for one person to achieve, so dividing work between at least two founders leads to faster milestone achievement. A technical co-founder and a CEO-type founder make a very strong starting team. A founder with a strong technical skill set can bring early versions of a product to customers to test assumptions about what the customer wants. The CEO-type founder can work to woo early customers, raise money, and build the startup team. Of course, any combination of these skill sets that moves the startup forward will work.

- **Other Key Team Positions.** For early stage startups, angels look for a minimum of two competent cofounders. If there are gaps in the team, they are generally filled as the startup grows and learns more about its market. Roles such as Chief Financial Officer (CFO) and VP of Sales and Marketing can be partially filled along the way by paying consultants to provide these services until full-time roles become affordable.

Pro Tip

Do You Need Traditional Titles?

Some startups want to eliminate the traditional layers of an organization, doing away with the CEO and other traditional C-level titles. As fun and anti-establishment a title such as Chief Bit Wrangler might sound, don't go there. You are trying to build credibility with investors, not provide a reason for them to say no to your pitch.

Large Target Market Size

When you're preparing your pitch for investors, be prepared to address the market for your product or service, particularly its size. Investors like startups that solve big problems. Dig up as many statistics as you can to demonstrate the following about your target market:

- **Large and Growing Market.** The estimated market size for your startup's product or service needs to be large for investors to be motivated.

- **Competitors' Share Considered.** The size of your target market needs to be large enough for several competitors to share. If your startup can grow to a 10% share of a $250 million total market, a revenue projection of $25 million annually sounds credible.

- **Dominate a Niche Market.** The market segment that you go after can be a niche of a larger ecosystem, but that niche needs to be big enough to support your revenue projections. Many startups focus on highly specialized niche markets, providing one-of-a-kind products or technology. This scenario can be interesting to angel investors.

- **Market Size and Financial Projections.** The market you describe to investors needs to appear to be sufficiently large enough to support your financial projections. Your revenue projections need to be realistic, showing believable market share assumptions. If you projections require a 50% market share to hit your year three projections, investors are not likely to let go of their cash.

  So what is a realistic market share assumption? That will in some part depend on the number of players in the market and its size. Generally speaking, if you look at the annual revenue projection for year 5, anything that exceeds 25% is probably unrealistic. To perform the calculation, divide market size by year 5 revenue (both in dollars); multiply the resulting decimal value by 100 (if your spreadsheet program doesn't do if for you) to arrive at the projected market share percentage. If your revenue projections have you capturing a significantly large percentage of the total available market for your product, then you likely need to rethink your projections. It is extremely rare for a startup to capture more than a quarter of a market in only five years.

Disruptive Technology or Ideas

Investors like the idea of new technology that upsets or dramatically changes an industry or market segment. With dramatic change comes dramatic opportunity to make money.

Disruptive technology is often very unkind to the existing players who have built their companies on the previous technology. For example, digital cameras emerged as a new and effective technology, knocking down competitors such as Kodak, who could not transition quickly enough from film photography to digital.

Napster, along with other peer-to-peer file sharing software and services, is another example of disruptive technology. Instead of consumers buying CDs by favorite bands, consumers could simply download the music from the Internet for free. Because this constituted digital piracy, Napster was shut down, paving the way for legitimate ways to buy music online, either through services such as iTunes that enable you to purchase and download digital music tracks, fee-based services that enable you to stream the music (and now movies) that you select, or ad supported platforms such as Pandora.

Like Napster, some new technology is so different, entrepreneurs and investors don't initially know how to make money with the new technology. The investor wants to play a part in the disruption, with the hope that the revenue model can be figured out and everybody in the game will make money.

Vitamins vs. Pain Killers

Investors look for companies that solve serious problems. The analogy of vitamins vs. painkillers comes up frequently. You take vitamins occasionally because it's a good idea, you take painkillers because you hurt and need to stop the pain now. Is your product merely a vitamin to the customers, or a painkiller? Painkillers are in much higher demand.

Customer Traction

Customer traction is a startup's way of saying you have paying customers. You have launched your product and customers are buying, or signing up as users. Here are a number of customer related factors that angels weigh when considering whether or not to invest in your startup:

- **Startup Cure All.** Having paying customers is a near cure all fore whatever else might hold a startup back from raising angel funding. Inexperienced founders, marginal market understanding, weak or no IP—all these shortcomings start to get downplayed or ignored by angels if you have lots of users or customers buying what you make.

- **Early Adopter Customers.** For most startups, quickly getting your product in the hands of five or 10 prospective customers is the number one priority. The product features might not be stabilized yet, but interested customers can engage and give you feedback. Early adopter customers are often signed up to adopt your product either for free or at a large discount to encourage participation. Build trust with potential investors by disclosing the details of early customer deals.

- **Customer Acquisition Process.** Investors also look at your sales and marketing process for getting new customers. Do you have to spend large amounts of time and money to sign up a new customer, or is it an easy sale? Products with a long or challenging sales cycle appeal less to investors.

- **Social/Viral Customer Uptake.** Investors like the idea that you can spread the word about your product through social and other viral channels, without major marketing investment. Be candid and transparent with investors about the level of effort (and any cost) required to push marketing initiatives such as blogging, social media posts, and other social marketing avenues.

- **Crowdfunding Success.** Crowd funding sites like Kickstarter.com and IndieGoGo.com can be a great way for startups to get early customers. Completing a successful crowd funding campaign is a strong validation of the market for a new product. Many startups prove their model, test pricing, and get customer feedback on product features using crowdfunding sites, and then seek angel investors to help fund the next stages of the company's growth.

 Early Customer Engagement

Angels like startups that engage early with prospective customers. When customers help define features that matter most to them, the startup has a much higher chance of growing sales and success.

Defensible IP or Market Position

Investors look for all possible ways to protect their investments. Patents and other forms of intellectual property can increase investor confidence in a startup's prospects. Ensuring that one or more of the following protective factors applies to your product helps pave the way for investment:

- **Defensible Intellectual Property.** Your startup has innovative technology or ideas, and you've filed for patents, trademarks, or trade secrets to prevent competitors from stealing your designs.

- **Patents.** While many investors like a startup with already patented technology, patents do not prevent competitors from entering the market. If the market is big enough, other established companies and startups will attempt to find ways around your patents, and launch their own versions of the idea. Owning a patent gives the startup the offensive right to stop others from using the same technology. Offensive right means that the startup has to take action to stop the infringing competitor—typically a cease and desist action or full-blown lawsuit.

- **First To Market.** Being the first product to market can interest angels, because it gives you the opportunity to makes sales and build the customer base prior to having competition. Many other factors need to be aligned however; the market must be large, you need proof that customers care and will pay, and investors have to believe you are capable of executing and surviving fast paced startup growth.

- **Network Effect.** Say you launch a new social network (think Facebook) and customers are signing up by the thousands because their friends have signed up. The network effect demonstrates that people will adopt your product via word of mouth, a powerful selling point for potential investors.

High Growth Potential (Three to Five Years)

The projected revenues of your startup need to be large enough to be interesting to angel investors. General ranges for startup revenue size, in three to five years are:

Small. Annual revenue less than $20 million per year

Medium. Annual revenue $20 to $50 million per year

Large. Revenues more than $100 million per year

The size of your annual revenues (and profits) implies possible exit valuation, and large exit valuations are how investors get the high returns on their money. Let's break it down:

- **10 to 20 Million.** Generally, angel investors look for startups that can reach annual revenues of at least $10 to $20 million or more, within three to five years. At these exit values an early stage investor is likely to get a decent multiple of their original investment in the startup.

- **Revenues to Exits.** Startup exit values are expressed as multiples of their annual revenues (or profits). For example, Startup A has a 3X exit on $25 million revenue, or a total of a $75 million exit value. (Potential acquirers generally pay a wide range of multiples for startups, 2X to 6X annual revenue are common.)

- **Why Three to Five Years?** It takes startups several years to bring their product to market, build its team, get exposed to the customer base, and finally start making money. The three to five (or seven) year timeframe is the normal amount of time it takes a startup to reach its stride. Figure 2 shows a typical chart of startup revenue projections.

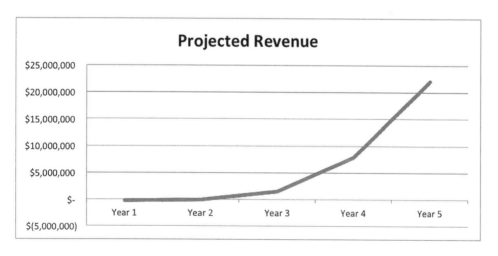

Figure 2. Projected revenues for most startups are low for the first several years.

Even Smaller Successes Can Be Win/Win: Not every exit has to be enormous to be a success for both founders and investors. Depending on the amount of investment needed to build the company to the exit event, a return of less than three times or on a smaller dollar scale such as if the angel investor(s) can get $1.5 million back on a $500,000 investment, is still a win. An independent angel might be willing to accept smaller returns on his or her investment due to a personal connection with the entrepreneur. See the following Small Success Walkthrough for an example.

Small Success Walkthrough

Niche startup has $3 million in revenue annually.

1. Startup gets acquired for 3X this annual revenue, or a $9 million exit.

2. Angels put in $300,000 on a pre-money valuation of $600,000, thus adding their capital to result in a post-money valuation of $900,000. In this scenario, the angels now own 33% ($300K+$600K=$900K, $300K is 33% of the $900K). No VCs were needed.

3. The startup is later acquired for $9 million dollars. The angel share of exit is $3,000,000, or 10 times the original investment. This is a home run for the angel investors.

Pro Tip

Massive User Base, No Revenue Model

Many Web tech startups are focused on creating a product that attracts millions of users, like Facebook, but they have not yet figured out how they will make money. Most angel investors are not very excited about this model for early stage startups. The risk is too high and too many things can go wrong. Your competitors could do a better job of adding new users, causing your site to lose traction.

Or, your infrastructure might be fragile and your site can't handle the traffic, so you lose users. While the millions of users model has worked for some startups, it's difficult to get angel investors to let go of cash for an all or nothing model.

Scalable Models

A startup must be able to overcome barriers to scale into a larger and stable business to attract angel investors. After large initial expenses such buying expensive equipment and building out your team to accommodate customer growth, capital and operational expenses should level out as revenue climbs.

Think of it in terms of how many dollars of revenue you expect to start getting for every dollar investment. Initially, that ratio might be $1:$1 or less. You need to ask whether your startup's business and revenue model enable it to scale up to meet large customer demand without having to add considerable resources (continue making large expenditures). Give realistic estimates of how expenses versus sales will lay out over time, and when you'll reach a sustainable ratio of expenses versus revenue growth, for example a ratio of $1:$3 or more. Figure 3 shows an example of a scalable business, where revenues continue to grow, and expenses level off.

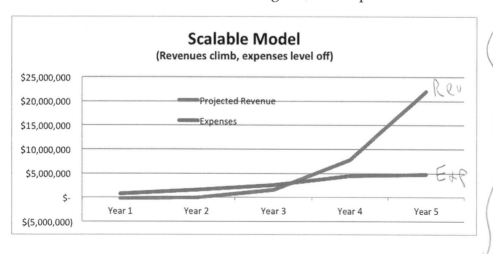

Figure 3. In Year 3, revenues grow and expenses level off.

Websites, SaaS plays, and mobile app startups are attractive because they usually scale very well. If the website or app backend architecture is carefully designed, adding large numbers of users does not require adding more head count or buying a room full of servers. A simple reconfiguring of the cloud servers (like Amazon EC2 infrastructure) addresses the need for a marginally low additional cost.

Are You All In?

Angels want to know that you are fully committed to the startup. At least one founder needs to be working on the startup full time. Investors know how much time is required to build a startup (full time, plus), and need to know the founders are able to commit the time required. You can't be working a day job and raise angel money. "I'll quit and dedicate full time to the startup when I get funded" does not fly. Other ways of demonstrating your all-in-ness include:

- You've made a personal financial investment in the startup.

- You've invested time in the startup. Product development work, coding, and design work all demonstrate commitment.

- Friends and family money has been invested.

- You have recruited talented co-founders and team members.

3

Startup Stages and Angel Investment

Angels look for startups on a continuum of risk reduction. What this means is that the more milestones a startup has achieved and continues to achieve, the less risk there is in the venture, because it is theoretically closer to success. An answer to the question "is this thing going to work?" is not as far off as it would be for a startup with few achievements.

As an entrepreneur seeking angel funding, you need to have enough progress in your startup to be interesting to angel investors. There are four overall stages in the startup company process. Understanding which stage your startup is at versus which stage investors are looking for can help you focus your efforts properly. Learn about the four stages and when you are likely to be ready to attract angel investment next.

Idea Stage

At the idea stage, your startup really consists of one or two founders and an idea. If any of the following statements apply to your startup, then it is likely still in the idea stage:

- The product or service is not yet developed; for example, prototyping or coding has not started

- Research or innovation is still in the lab.

- The idea has yet to be tested with prospective customers, and a revenue model might be unclear.

- The corporate entity may or may not be formed.
- You are developing the business plan (if required)

The Great Business Plan Mistake

If you are just at the idea stage, it's difficult to raise cash from experienced investors. A great idea and a business plan are not enough. Don't make the mistake of spending months writing a stellar business plan, only to have it rejected. A well thought out and well written business plan does not reduce enough risk for an angel to invest. More validations are needed—build a simple version of your product, get it in the hands of customers, and prove there is a demand.

- **Idea Stage Equity.** At the idea stage, equity in the startup is usually divided among the founders in some agreeable split. Figure 4 shows a 50/50 split of equity between two founders (of course, equity does not have to be split equally.) No outside investors are involved in this example.

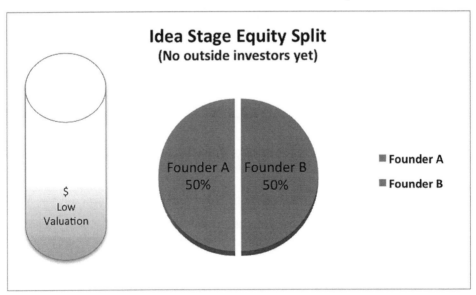

Figure 4. Idea stage equity is divided between two founders.

- **Valuation Low or Not Necessary.** At the idea stage, the valuation of the startup is expectedly low. Because typically few if any tasks have been executed to move the startup forward, no real need to actually put a valuation on the company exists. The need to establish a valuation arises later when an outside investment is being pursued.

- **Personal Funding.** Funding at the idea stage typically comes from the entrepreneur, with sources including personal savings, credit cards, or other opportunities such as pitch competitions. Friends and family money, government research funding such as Small Business Innovation Research (SBIR) grants, and occasionally independent angel investors can also fund the early steps at the idea stage.

If an investor invests at the stage, he or she is really placing a vote on the person, not the idea or the company.

Startup Stage

The startup stage comes next. Characteristics of the startup stage include:

- A product prototype or alpha has been developed and is being tested with potential customers.

- The startup team remains incomplete, with some key positions still unfilled.

- Some early sales revenue is possible, especially with Web and mobile products.

- Pivots are common. As you get feedback from early customers about your product, you are likely to change your product or target a different side of the market segment.

Here are additional factors that are typical at the startup stage:

- **Friends and Family Funding.** While funding at this stage typically comes from the founders along with friends and family, securing some level of angel investment at the startup stage is possible. Independent angels are more likely to invest at this stage, and such investments still represent more of a vote of confidence in the founder(s), more so than in the startup itself.

- **Startup Stage Equity.** At the startup stage, a few outside investors are likely to be supporting the ongoing efforts. Figure 5 shows a small percentage of equity (5%) carved out for a family member (Dad) who invested some cash in the venture. Note also that an option pool (15%) was allocated at this stage. These stock options will be used in the future as incentives for key employees. See section "Equity Stakes and Option Pools" for more details on stock options.

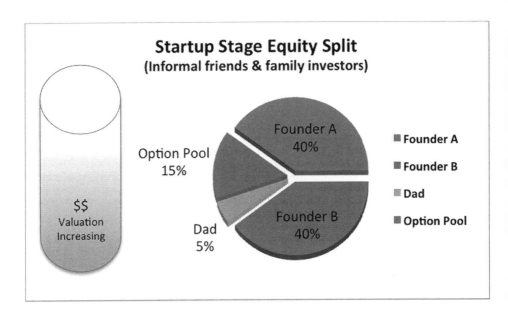

Figure 5. At the Startup stage, some equity may be given to friends and family.

- **Valuation Still Low, but Growing.** At the startup stage, the valuation of the startup is still low, but efforts toward building the product and proving it with customers are well underway. These accomplishments help increase the valuation of the startup, and with Dad as the first outside investor, a nominal valuation can be established. In the example illustrated by Figure 6, Dad was given 5% of the equity in exchange for his investment of a relatively small amount of cash, let's say $10,000. A quick look at the math shows the founders established a pre-money valuation of $190,000, add in Dad's $10,000 for a post-money valuation of $200,000. Dad's $10K bought him 5% of the equity ($10,000 investment/$200,000 post money = 5%.) Friends and Family funding rounds are usually on the order of a few to tens of thousands, but hey, some friends and family are richer than others, so any amount can be possible). Note also that an Option Pool was created to build in the equity structure for future key employees. See the section "Equity Stakes and Option Pools" for more details on Option Pools.

- **Pivots are Common.** At the startup stage it is common for founders to change directions in terms of the product, its features, or even the customer being targeted—these changes are called "pivots" in startup lingo, and are common at the startup stage. Investors want to see how potential customers like the prototype, beta, or test version of your innovation. Seasoned investors know that founders have a high likelihood of needing to pivot during the early stages of the startup. Founders are exploring the product fit with early customers, or beta testers. Pivoting to a new version of a product satisfies issues or feedback from the potential customers or partners. Adding or removing product features, changing functionality, or conceiving of completely new products all constitute pivots. Pivots cost time and money, but are a natural and essential part of the process of bringing new ideas to the world. (For more on product and market fit, consider starting to follow expert startup educator at Steve Blank, who frequently addresses this topic at his website www.steveblank.com.)

Traction Stage

Your startup moves to the traction stage when it consistently can acquire customers or users, a big milestone. Some startups, such as mobile app or Web-based products, can get to this stage very quickly and may not even need angel investment to do it. Other ventures clearly need investor cash to get to the early customer stage.

These characteristics further identify a business in the traction stage:

- Product features crystalize, with little or no additional pivoting.

- You have a base of customers using your product, with positive customer feedback.

- Not only are customers buying, but also they are returning for more, (known as customer/user retention)

- You have tested your pricing and revenue model and it seems to work.

- You understand the sales cycle, and are able to add new customers at a predictable cost

- You have probably filled gaps the in your startup team, with both a technical founder and a CEO-type founder on board.

- Your team starts to develop partnerships with other organizations and companies that can help you grow.

In addition, at the traction stage:

- **Customer Validation Drives the Traction Stage.** The validation that people want and are willing to pay for your product is the Holy Grail for investors. The closer you get to true paying customers, the less risk the angel perceives in the venture. Paying customers show that you have reduced the market risk associated with your venture. Other risks still exist, such as execution risk (your team's ability to build

44

the company and serve your customers), but with your team in place and aligned, it can make decisions and navigate setbacks and disasters.

- **Angels Start To Play and Valuation Grows.** At the traction stage, angel investors can talk to your paying customers, get a first hand view of the market segments you serve, and begin to assess the investment risks and potential rewards. Figure 6 shows an example equity split with an angel investment group owning a 25% stake in the startup. Note that the existing shareholders (the founders, Dad, and the option pool) have been diluted somewhat. The increasing valuation of the startup offsets the dilution—the pie is getting bigger, and everybody is benefiting from the accomplishments fueled by the angel investments.

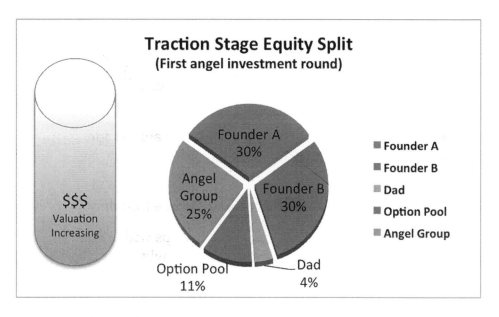

Figure 6. An example equity split when angel investors come into play.

Growth Stage

A few years into your startup roadmap, success in your target market drives the need for additional funding to fuel growth of the organization. This is the growth stage, also characterized by:

- A solid base of customers or users purchase your product.

- Customer or user demand creates the need for money for growth.

- Your product or service is widely available.

- The business generates ongoing revenues and should be close to cash flow positive.

- Growing revenues and leveling off expenses show the benefits of your scalable business model.

- New product ideas or line extensions are in the development pipeline and being tested.

No gaps remain in your team, with organizational processes stabilizing.

Even though at the growth stage your startup likely has already taken on some level of outside investment (angel funds, loans, friends and family money), you may need to go back to the well to fund further business expansion. Going back to the angels or VCs for additional capital because your company is growing is a good problem to have. Figure 7 shows an example equity split with VCs owning 30% of the company. (The first investment into a startup by a VC is typically called a "Series A Round.") Once again, the VC investment dilutes existing shareholders' stakes, but valuation should have increased, and with luck, the company is becoming interesting to potential exit partners.

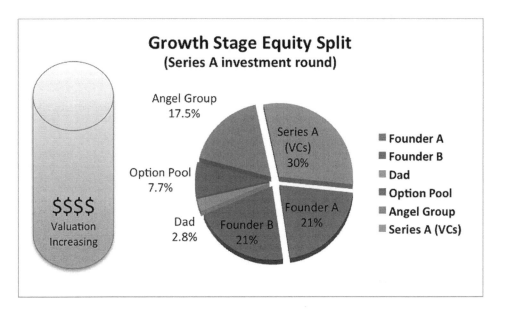

Figure 7. At the growth stage, VCs can get interested and the equity pie is fragmented.

Investors in growth stage startups look at historical metrics of your company. Months, if not years, of actual financial data are available, and investors want to know:

- How efficiently have you used the capital you've received?

- How well have you controlled expenses?

- Are you at or close to a break-even level of sales/revenue?

- Are there major infrastructure costs needed to serve an ever larger number of customers, or has the startup operation reached an expense plateau while retaining the ability to scale up to meet the intake of thousands more customers?

4

Setting Your Funding Target and Plan

Once you have an understanding of the match between startup stage and the interest level of angel investors, determining how much money to raise and creating a detailed funding plan is the next step. This section provides an overview of this process.

In 2013, the median angel or angel group investment round ranged from $500,000 to $700,000, but angel rounds can be as small as $10,000, or as high as $2 million or more. Different startups have different funding needs:

- **Money Raising Stages.** Many startups raise funding in stages. The founders convince investors to take the high risk in the early stages of the venture, using the investment to create proof that there is a market for what the startup has to offer. Then the founders raise additional funding rounds, with the subsequent funds used to advance the startup to profitability and hopefully an exit.

- **Low Cost Startups.** Some Web startups can be launched and attract paying customers for very little invested capital. Keep the founders fed and housed for a few months, and they can produce a good looking product and get it in the hands of users. (This is the concept of startup accelerators like Y Combinator and Techstars).

- **High Cost Startups.** Other startups require much more capital. Medical devices, biotech products, and nanotechnology materials can require millions to get early product testing stages completed. Offsetting these high

49

startup costs is the size of the market opportunity. Medical and biotech markets tend to be huge, and angels are willing to take a gamble for potential super high return on the investment.

Determining How Much to Raise

The following steps offer a generalized sequence for determining how much your startup needs to raise:

1. **Build a Roadmap.** Determine the rough phases of your startup roadmap. Include major milestones that when achieved increase the valuation of the company.

2. **Estimate Development Budget.** Make educated guesses about the budget/funding needed to complete the sub tasks in each phase of the roadmap.

3. **Calculate Burn Rate.** Make estimates about the ongoing monthly expenses needed to keep the startup alive during the phases outlined in your roadmap.

4. **Develop Pre-Money Valuation.** Complete a pre-money valuation exercise to put an estimate on what your startup is worth at the beginning of the implementation phase. (Section "Valuation Methods" provides an overview of ways to estimate your startup valuation.)

5. **Sanity Check.** Compare the valuation estimate to the total funding needed to reach the major milestones. Is it reasonable? Will you have to give up too much equity to raise this amount? If the amount you need to raise is more than one half of your valuation estimate, consider raising smaller amounts from non-equity sources (such as friends and family), using this money to hit more milestones and increase your valuation prior to raising angel investment.

Distilling a Funding Plan

Once you've made good guesses about the investment needed to reach significant milestones, create a detailed use of funds document that details your assumptions for investors.

Your use of funds plan should include:

- How much have you invested so far?
- How much will you need for this round?
- When you will need it?
- What you are going to use the money for, that is, which milestones will the investment enable you to hit?
- When will you need additional investment, or can you reach a self-sustaining level of cash flow?

Raise Amount and Multiple Angels

Many startups pursuing angel investment will need to raise money from more than one angel or angel group. If you are raising $250,000 or $500,000, you are likely to need investments from at least a few sources.

Many angel groups and independent angels have limits on the amount they put into a company. Amounts such as $50,000, $75,000, or $100,000 from one group is typical, so to get to a number like $500,000, plan on wooing a few angels or groups.

Raising Too Little Money

Trying to raise small amounts of money, (such as $10,000-$50,000) from angels signals a mismatch between your goals/initiatives and the perceived amount of money needed to fund the initiatives. "You'll need more money to do that… " is a common angel comment. Raising too little shows you don't yet understand your market or business model, and have more work to do.

Asking for small amounts of investment from outsiders implies one of two things: either you are willing to give up a tiny amount of equity for the small amount of investment, or your pre-money valuation is quite low.

Raising Too Much Money

Experienced entrepreneurs know that startups always need more money and more time. As long as your valuation supports it, raise as much money as you can in a round. If you find that your startup is exciting to angels and their money is flowing, raise as much as you can, and then spend it like it was your last dime. Going "back to the well" for more money takes time and introduces new problems. Your time is better spent bringing your product to customers and making it better.

Arriving at a Valuation

If investors are interested in investing in your startup, the conversation will eventually lead to valuation. Valuation refers to the total worth or dollar value placed on the startup at the time of a money raise. The valuation is largely accepted/agreed on by the outside investor, but the startup's founders (and advisors) should determine a starting point valuation. Two key terms are associated with startup company valuations:

- **Pre-money valuation:** How much your company is valued at before an investment round.

- **Post-money valuation:** How much the company is valued after the investment round.

Figure 8 illustrates how these terms fit together.

Figure 8. Adding up the post-money valuation.

Also keep these opposing considerations in mind when considering how to value your company:

- Investors want low pre-money valuations, so their investment buys are larger percentage of equity.

- Founders want higher pre-money valuations, so they give up less equity when investment rounds close.

Determining the pre-money valuation of a startup is a combination of real and perceived measures.

Numerous factors influence the perceived value piece, including:

- **Market Size.** How big is the market the startup is going after?

- **Size of the Company.** What are the revenue projections over the next three to five years?

- **Intellectual Property (IP).** Does the startup have significant IP or other high competitive barrier advantages?

- **Founders and Team.** How experienced is the founding team? Have they worked on a startup before, or is this their first go?

- **Product/Service or Technology.** Is it revolutionary and disruptive, or merely evolutionary?

- **Traction.** Do you have customers or users? At what rate can you add new ones?

- **Amount Already Invested.** How much money has already been invested, and how much time in terms of development, research, or innovation?

- **Stage of the Startup.** What stage of development is the startup at: idea/business plan, product developed and tested, or other?

- **Competition.** What is the competition like in the sector of the startup?

- **Need for Addition Investment.** Does the startup need a significant amount of additional cash to reach its goals?

See the later section "Valuation Methods" to learn about more specific techniques for valuing your startup.

Valuation Relative To How Much to Raise

The amount of funding you seek must also make sense in relationship to your pre-money valuation. Consider the equation:

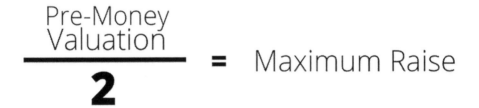

$$\frac{\text{Pre-Money Valuation}}{2} = \text{Maximum Raise}$$

Figure 9. Figuring the maximum you can raise based on valuation.

Dividing your pre-money valuation by two gives you a good ballpark limit for how much you can raise in a particular funding round. The math works out so that the investor would own 33% of the equity after the investment. Note this is a simplified guideline. Option pools and other factors can dramatically change the ownership math.

Valuation Pitfall

If you don't think through the valuation in relation to how much you are trying to raise, angels may question your rationale. For example, say you are seeking to raise $250,000 for 5% of the company. This implies a valuation of $5 million (20 x $250,000 = $5 million). For most raw startups, a valuation of $5 million is high and such a small stake for such a high dollar angel investment is too low. Be sure to do the simple math.

Equity Stakes and Option Pools

Giving up some equity in your startup is required to raise funds to build and grow. Equity given to angels in exchange for investment typically ranges from 10% to 30% in early stage startups.

In addition using equity to secure angel funding, most startups create an option pool of common stock shares. Use option pool shares to sweeten compensation deals for key employees and reduce the amount of cash outlaid for salaries. Employees with stock options hope to share in the potential success of the startup. Stock options are a form of compensation, so the option holder must consider the tax implications. Option pool sizes are typically 10% to 20% of the total equity of the company. A startup may also use options instead of cash to secure services for the startup, with paying lawyers and financial consultants in this way being the most common.

Experienced startup founders know that they have to share the pie to get investors, and that sharing dilutes the percentage ownership the founders retain. Getting diluted is just a part of the game of startups. Founders' percentage ownership declines, but the overall pie is getting bigger. Angel investor cash infusions help the startup reach critical milestones and grow revenues, which directly results in the valuation of the startup increasing—the pie is getting bigger. Figure 10 shows a graphical example of an early stage equity split.

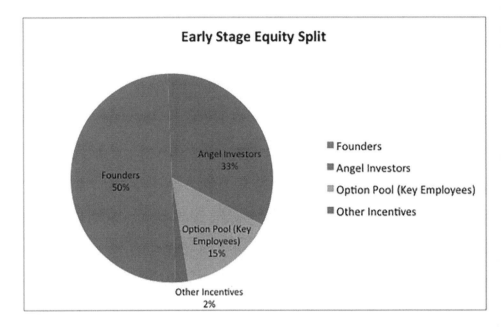

Figure 10. A example early stage equity split with an option pool established.

Investment Walk-Through

Consider the following investment scenario, showing how valuation and raise amount are loosely linked.

1. Pre-money valuation of $1,000,000.

2. Founders desire to raise $500, 000 and give up no more than 33% of the company equity during the angel rounds.

3. Pre-money: $1,000,000, added to…

4. Investment: $500,000, equals…

5. Post-money: $1,500,000 valuation.

6. The investor owns 33% of the company ($500K/$1,500K). Figure 10 above shows a graphic view of the startup ownership. If the funding plan created by the startup calls for a larger investment amount, either the founders give up more equity, or a higher pre-money valuation needs to be negotiated.

5

The Angel Funding Process

While every angel deal has its unique flow, overall you can expect to go through several stages in the angel funding process. This section walks you through those stages, including giving you more details about what you need to prepare when and what your goals should be at particular points along the way.

Stage 1. Introduction to Angels

Warm Referral

Whether you are seeking an independent angel or an angel group, it is best to get a warm referral. Connect with someone who is either a member of the angel group, or a well respected affiliate of the group. Have your supporter make the introduction to the group's organizer. Once you are connected, submit your business plan or summary documents to the angel or angel group.

Many groups use websites such as gust.com to help organize the screening and submission process. Sites like Gust enable entrepreneurs to upload documents and videos, so angels can review, rate, and discuss startups with in their group.

Startup Review

Angels review your plan or pitch deck and decide if they want you to pitch the group in person.

Invitation to Pitch

If the angel or angel group is intrigued by your startup, you get invited to pitch.

What You Need To Have Ready

- Executive Summary
- Business Plan
- Financial Model
- Current Status and Key Milestones
- Use of Funds
- Valuation
- Other Validations, For Example Customers

Key Goals at the Introduction Stage

Get invited to the in-person pitch. You want to meet the angels, get to know them, and let your passion and personality shine through.

Key Hot Buttons at the Introduction Stage

- Your product solves an understandable problem.

- You can demonstrate that you have a large and reachable market.

- Customers are willing to pay for your product, or the user base is growing fast.

- Your team looks okay on the surface.

- The angels understand and can work comfortably with your market/industry—Web, mobile, biotech, and so on.

- The valuation you present falls within the acceptable range for the angel or group.

Stage 2. The Pitch

Meeting Date Set

Most organized angel groups meet monthly. Angels will inform you of the meeting date and the time slot when they'd like you to make your pitch.

Prep Your Champion

If you have a champion in the angel group, prep that person on your pitch approach and other key topics such as your raise amount, valuation, and progress toward key milestones. You might also ask your champion to make your introduction to the group. Other angels in the group are likely unfamiliar with you and your startup and knowing that "one of their own" brought you to the angel group often paves the way for your pitch.

Get to Know The Angels

Either prior to your pitch presentation, or after, take the time to briefly get to know some of the angels. Follow up on a question asked during your pitch, or offer your business card or product samples (if applicable) to start short discussions. Your goal at every opportunity is to build trust and share your passion for your startup—brief conversations contribute towards this goal.

Make Your Pitch

Your presentation to the group usually should be no more than 15 minutes, with 15 minutes of questions. (Formats vary. Some angel groups are very casual, while others have a more set routine.) If your pitch presentation is longer than 15 minutes, you need to distill it down more. Practice it over and over again until it flows well and seems natural. Avoid reading from note cards, and attempt to make your presentation style conversational, meaning that you are just talking, not delivering a speech.

Q&A

Once you have completed your pitch and opened the discussion for questions, angels will probe and poke holes in your plan/story/ideas. The idea of the pitch is to pique their interest, and a healthy level of questions is exactly what you want. If angels want to know more, that indicates at least some level of interest. Also be prepared for questions *during* your pitch. Small groups may be very informal and just want to ask questions as you present. Be flexible, but keep the pitch moving along if this happens.

The Vote

Organized angel groups may either vote during the pitch meeting regarding whether or not to move on to due diligence or wait and let you know later.

If you are pitching to an independent angel, and feel that the conversation is coming to a close, be sure to "ask for the order," asking the angel if there is enough interest for him or her to make an investment. There are of course several potential answers to this question: "I need more information," "It's not the right fit for my investment plans," "You are not far enough along yet and need more progress toward paying customers," and the ultimate "Yes indeed, I want to invest in your startup, when can we close the deal?"

What You Need To Have Ready

- Bring your presentation or pitch deck created in the tool of your choice—PowerPoint, Prezi, and so on—along with any equipment needed, such as a projector, printouts, product samples, and other business summary documents that you might want to leave with the angels.

- Be sure your pitch is well practiced, yet personable and conversational in style. (That is, if you simply "read" your pitch, it will fall flat and project a lack of preparation.)

- Be sure to cover how much you are trying to raise, and give a simple use of funds explanation.

Backup Information To Have on Hand

- Valuation and basis for it

- Sales pipeline showing the customer you have in your sales process

- Key milestones, including product development timelines, and so on

- Gaps and how you plan to fill them

- Clear revenue model, proven by early customers

- A list of other Angel groups and contact that have pitched to

- How much have raised already, including investments by you, your team, and friends and family

Key Goals at the Pitch Stage

- Get the angel group to agree to move on to due diligence.

- Build credibility and trust with the angels.

- Share your passion so that the angels can see you will be an engaged, energetic partner.

Key Hot Buttons at the Pitch Stage

- Demonstrate clear customer interest in your product.

- Identify your defendable market position: IP, trade secrets, first to market, and so on.

- Show that the management team knows the process of raising startup capital.

- Communicate how the angel investment would make a clear impact towards achieving the startup's milestone and clearly increase the valuation of the company beyond just the cash infused.

- In three to five years, the projected revenue of the company will be large enough for a profitable exit for the angels.

Rookie Mistake—the NDA

DO NOT ask angel investors to sign your Non-Disclosure Agreement (NDA). They won't do it, and asking makes you look like an amateur. If you have something sensitive and proprietary, simply do not provide details that would compromise your IP. If your discussions with investors get to the point that they request deep technical due diligence, then you can request an NDA to be signed.

Stage 3. Due Diligence

At the due diligence stage of the angel funding process, angels dig into your startup plans and documents and assess and confirm more details about your startup. Some angels opt to do very little due diligence on a startup. The startup founders might be at the very early stages of the venture, a time with little to dig into. In such a case, angels trust their gut and the founders. Angel groups often form due diligence committees and dig deep, examining and questioning the many areas and assumptions of the company. Due diligence is also a time for the angels to get to know the entrepreneurs and their team, getting a feel for personalities, and how the founders work together, who takes the lead, and so on.

Due diligence can take time (several weeks), sometimes by design. Investors want to see how you do at hitting the milestones you said you would.

Testing Assumptions

Angels will test and validate (or in cases invalidate) your key assumptions. For example, what happens to the startup's revenue if you don't get a major customer? Or, what happens to your launch plans if your Web developer misses the project completion milestones? Having a plan B to offer can provide more confidence in key assumptions.

The full gamut of what due diligence could entail includes:

Market Assessment

- Market segments and structure

- Go to market strategy

- Method for reaching customers

- Sales pipeline and sales process

- Early customer interviews—validate the need, willingness to pay, comments on competition

- Customers lost and reasons why

- Sales cycle—long, short, terms of payment

- Competition and competitive strengths and weaknesses

Technology Assessment

- Status of technology development
- Testing and customer feedback
- Licensing agreements needed and executed
- Third-party expert review of technology
- Status of patents, trademarks, and other branding
- Technology partners and their level of engagement

Management Team Assessment

- Get to know the personalities of the founders
- Full resumes of founders and team
- Online profile reviews—LinkedIn, Facebook, and so on
- Business reference checks, background checks
- Levels of team commitment and passionate
- Whether the team is coachable
- Gaps or critical needs in the team

Operations Assessment

- R&D staffing, customer engagement staff
- Sales process and expertise
- Marketing messaging and elements, such as website
- Accounting and information systems

Legal Review

- Corporate legal entity—LLC, C corporation, S corporation
- Bylaws or operating agreement review

- Existing investment terms review

- Lawsuits or other legal actions

- IP details—patents, trademarks, and so on

Financial Review

- Financial model review, testing of assumptions

- Revenues and costs

- Cash flow, including major outlays needed, seasonality issues

- Funding plan with key milestones

- Capitalization table review

- Current valuation and justification

- Follow-on capital needs; more rounds?

- Previous investors and terms

- Realistic possibility of an exit

Key Goals at the Due Diligence Stage

- Be completely transparent

- Be patient, but be sure to follow up to clarify any questions or requests

- Focus on making progress and reporting that progress to the angels.

- Mind your startup's sales pipeline, user uptake, burn rate, and other key metrics.

Stage 4. Investment

The Deal Details

- Your startup and the angels discuss the deal structure:

    o Whether the angels will receive equity, convertible debt, preferred shares, etc.

    o The amount to be invested

    o Board seat for the angels

    o If an equity deal, a valuation is agreed on, as well as the percentage of the company to owned by the angels

    o Milestones to be hit and whether the investment will be released in tranches at key milestones

- The angels will typically offer a term sheet with the investment details and investor rights and preferences.

- Your startup and the angels agree on final deal terms.

- Lawyers from each side will review and finalize the legal agreements needed to close the investment.

- The founders and angels sign the legal documents, and you get a check.

What You Need To Have Ready

- Your startup team must be in complete alignment. Is everybody clear and in agreement about the terms of the investment, equity ownership consequences, and commitment?

- The founders' lawyer should have reviewed the legal documents prepared by the angels' lawyers. (See the later section "Legal Documents Pertaining to Angel Funding" for an overview of startup funding legal documents.) Most angel investment deals include stipulations that the startup is responsible for the legal fees associated with the investment round.

Key Goals at the Investment Stage

- Both sides must agree on a reasonable valuation.

- The founders should see clear "more than money" value from engaging with the angels.

- Put the money in the bank—never assume the deal is done until this point.

Stage 5. Keeping Investors Updated

Provide Written Updates

Once you get the money in the bank, you'll need to keep your investors updated on your progress. Most angel groups meet once per month to discuss the status of the companies they've invested in. Providing them a brief update document or email prior to each monthly meeting shows that you are organized and fulfilling your part of the relationship between founder and investor.

What to Report—The Short List

- **Headlines.** Lead off with short status updates about major initiatives, milestones missed or hit, major customers or partnership opportunities.

- **Technology/Product Development.** Share the status of product development, testing results, beta tests, IP opportunities, setbacks or leaps ahead.

- **Financial Condition.** Cover the key financial metrics, including actual versus forecasted revenues, cash on hand, current burn rate, monthly and year-to-date revenues compared to your forecast. Also note any major changes to expenses and progress toward break-even.

- **Funding/Capital Raising.** If additional fundraising rounds are underway, provide the status of fund raising goals and activities and whether there are issues, concerns, or major changes.

- **Human Resources.** Share details about compensation discussions, stock option plans, hiring/firing decisions, and so on.

- **Sales and Marketing.** Detail key customers landed, important opportunities, major marketing initiatives, and other activities that influence the sales success of the company.

- **Shareholder/Investor Relations.** Provide board meeting schedules, and give advanced notice on significant issues that need to be addressed by the investors, such as raising additional money.

How Long Does It Take to Raise Money?

The founders should expect to spend a significant amount of time raising money. You need to pitch multiple angel groups and independent angels. Numerous meetings, phone calls, customer visits, and document prep time will consume your time.

Whiles some funding deals can come together in a few weeks, investor-ready founders should expect 3 to 6 months to close a funding deal. Here are a few additional factors that influence a fundraising timeline:

- **Getting to Know You.** Both independent angels and

organized angel groups want to get to know you. What is your personality? How do you make decisions? How do you interact with your team? How do you manage setbacks? It takes time for angels to get a sense of the answers to such questions about each founder's operating style. It could take up to three months for an organized angel group to feel they know you well enough to pull the trigger on an investment. Until then, help them continue the due diligence of getting to know you, your team, and your users or customers.

- **Fast Independent Angels.** Independent angels with experience in startup investing can be very quick to invest. If they know and like you and like the stage your startup is at, you could have a check in the bank overnight. This is rare, however.

- **Slower Angel Groups.** Organized angel groups tend to be slower to invest and carry out their review processes. Their steps for evaluating startups take more time and many angel groups meet once per month, reducing the opportunities to meet founders, hear pitches, and perform due diligence. Angel groups also tend to have more deals in their pipeline to evaluate, creating a rationing of their limited time.

- **Funding Timeline.** Founders should sketch out a funding timeline that includes their estimates for the time needed to raise the capital needed and outline a plan B if funding is slower to materialize or not at all. Many startups survive lean times by bootstrapping, founders taking on consulting gigs, and other creative ways to keep the startup alive and hitting milestones.

- **Personal Financial Runway.** In addition to estimating a timeline for your fund raising efforts, founders should estimate how long their personal financial runway is. It's important to be "eyes wide open" about your personal financial set up. Are you putting everything on the line with this startup? Have you quit your job and intend to live on savings while you pursue your startup? Will mortgages go unpaid if you fail? Making a personal budget for yourself and your family is an absolute necessity. And if you have a spouse or significant other, take the time to get agreement on how far you can go without an income. What is plan B if angel funds do not materialize? Do you have enough money to cover your personal needs and keep the business alive while you raise angel capital?

6

Is Your Startup "Investor Ready"?

The term investor ready means two things:

1. That you have thought through the key areas of your startup and created some kind of documentation that you can provide investors that answer many of the questions that any investor will eventually ask. For example, what does your startup do, is it solving a large problem for a specific customer base, how big is your market, what does you team look like, how are you better or at least different from your competitors, and so on.

2. Your startup has achieved certain key milestones that take the risk out of your new venture, helping investors feel more confident about your chances of success and a possible return on their invested capital.

The following sections review the key documents that well prepared startups use to help answer these questions.

Business Plans

Old School Business Plans. The old-school idea of investor-ready meant that you had written a business plan. Everybody asks for one, or tells the entrepreneur to go write one, and few investors actually read them. The problem with business plans is they are like historical records, they are static or backward looking, and do not tell what you plan to do going forward in the future.

Startups are Experiments. Startups that investors are interested in risking money in offer something new, something that has not been done before. Investors want innovation, disruption, and in general exciting new ideas being adopted by large numbers of customers. Therefore, startups are experiments. And as with many experiments, many unanswered questions exist. Only by creating a version of your product and testing it with actual customers can you answer many of the key questions. Do customers understand your product, does it solve a big problem for them, and are they willing to pay for it? Creating a traditional business plan assumes that you know all of these answers.

Investors don't invest in a startup because of a great business plan alone. Avoid the temptation to spend large amounts of time writing a business plan, but instead, spend that time creating an early version of your product and testing it with customers. The following steps illustrate how this can go wrong:

The Wrong Way:

1. Have a great idea.

2. Write a business plan.

3. Try to get investors to fund the startup.

4. Start building your product.

5. See if anybody wants what you built.

This sequence inevitably crashes and burns at Step 3—get investors. Investors do not invest in ideas and business plans, they invest in startup teams that create products and prove customers care and are willing to pay. Some investors have set the bar high, claiming that you don't really have a company until you have paying customers.

A more successful sequence is outlined in the following steps:

The Right Way:

1. Have a great idea.

2. Build an early version of your product.

3. See if anybody wants what you built.

4. If #3 looks good, write a business plan (or sub set documents as detailed below)

5. Try to get investors to help fund the next phase of your startup.

There are however, times that you will need to create a complete and traditional business plan:

- **Business plan competitions.** Many economic development organizations such as county or regional or state level non-profits charged with the mission of supporting and growing small business hold business plan competitions and offer attractive prize money for the best plans. Some prizes, typically in the form of a grant, are in the $10,000 to $50,000 range—a significant win for a small startup.

- **A prospective investor asks for one.** There are many experienced angel investors that expect a startup to have jumped the hurdle of creating a full business plan. If you are beginning discussions with a potential investor and you believe they would be a good fit (an advocate and supporter, more than money) with your company, it might be worth the time to create a full business plan.

Whether you believe in writing traditional business plans or not, investors will need to know what your startup does and why it is investable, so you'll need to write it down or document it somehow. Ultimately, you must be able to *send and show* investors something. Whether you are meeting investors in person, or uploading documents to an angel group website, you need to send investors documents to read over lunch or on the plane.

The following sections outline the key investor ready documents and tools that relate the story and progress of your startup.

Your Funding Pitch and Pitch Deck

Investor ready founders have prepared (and practiced) a great 10 to 15 minute pitch. The pitch gets investors and supporters excited about your startup, and answers high level questions. The purpose of the pitch is to interest investors enough that they want to know more—you don't need to tell them everything in your pitch.

There are many approaches to an investor pitch, with the traditional outline pitch and the more Hollywood styled "story pitch" flavors being the most used by founders.

- **The Traditional Pitch.** Many investors expect this tried and true approach. If you can deliver the pitch with passion and clarity, you will do well selling your startup to investors. A traditional pitch is presented in the following flow:

    o **The Problem.** What is the problem you solve?

    o **Your Solution.** What is your solution to the problem, and why is it special?

    o **Customers.** Who do you solve a problem for, and why do they care?

    o **Market.** How big is the market, how many ideal customers are in it?

    o **Business Model.** How do you interact with customers, and how do you make money?

    o **Your Team.** Why are you the right team?

    o **Technology.** Do you have a secret sauce?

    o **Intellectual Property.** Have you protected your technology?

- o **Competition.** Who are your competitors, what are your advantages?

- o **Financial Projections.** What are your projected revenues, costs, and expenses?

- o **Funding Needs and Uses.** How much are you raising, and what milestones will it help you reach?

- **The Story Pitch.** This style of pitch tells a great story for investors to follow. It is less rigid and business-school-like than the traditional pitch. If you are fortunate to have paying customers when you are pitching to investors, your story pitch tells how you got there, how you engaged early with customers and pivoted to a product that really matters to your customers, how much your customers now love your product, and how you are poised for tremendous growth (with the help of a little investor cash). If you are pre-customer, your story pitch is focused on selling the idea of you product, how potential customers will use it, and how you will use investment funds to get there. For either path, build a short story that you can tell with passion and that leaves investors wanting to know more.

- **Email-able Pitch Deck vs. an In-Person Pitch Deck.** Experienced entrepreneurs create multiple versions of the pitch deck. One version is used for in-person presentations to investors. This version contains very simple slides, few words, and powerful images and graphics. The founder giving the pitch provides all the details verbally as s/he delivers the presentation. Another version of the pitch deck presents more details, text descriptions, and more slides. You can email the detailed pitch to investors, who can then easily read and understand the details without the founder needing to provide that information in person.

- **Pitch Duration.** Investor pitches should be 15 minutes or less. Investors hear hundreds of pitches, so 15 minutes feels like an eternity to impatient angels. Some pitch competitions limit the pitch time to eight minutes or even five minutes.

The idea of the pitch is to get investors interested enough to 1) understand what you do, 2) ask questions, 3) talk to you in more detail after the pitch.

Your Business Model and Revenue Model

Action-oriented founders fight the temptation to want to disregard all the jargon of startups, especially MBA-sounding terms like "business model." It's better to resist the temptation and know what you will be quizzed about, including your startup's business model. In plain English, your business model is a description of how your startup interacts with your customers and/or users, how you deliver your product/service, and how you ultimately make money.

- **Customers and Users.** While it might sound elementary, your customers are the ones who pay you. Many startups have both customers and users. Users are the people that use you product. Sometimes your customer and user are the same person/entity. Many times they are not, as for ad-supported smartphone apps, a common example of a business model with split customers/users. For example, you often can download and install smartphone games for free. The game player (the user) never has to pay a fee, but the game screen displays rolling advertisements for other products. The app developer makes money either directly from the advertisers/sponsors (the customer) or via complex mobile ad networks.

- **Revenue Model.** Often assumed to be part of a business model, your revenue model describes in detail how you make money. While a business model describes the flows of product or service and other interactions with your customers, your revenue model describes who pays you and how much and how often they pay.

Following are some common business and revenue models:

78

- **Direct to the end customer.** For example, you sell a product directly to customers via the Web, with no further support or contact. Customers pay via credit card or PayPal, or some other accepted method.

- **Brick and mortar retail via distributers.** You sell your product to/through distributors that then sell to retailers. Customers buy your products at the retail shop. The retailer pays the distributor, and the distributor pays you (typically deducting a distributor fee), often 30 to 60 days (or more) later.

- **Subscription.** Examples include digital newspapers or the wine-of-the-month club. Your customers receive your product on a regular schedule, and you charge for it monthly, yearly, or some other agreed-upon frequency.

- **Freemium.** These models give a basic version of the product away for free, but charge a monthly fee for more advanced and most desirable or premium features.

- **Razor and razor blades.** Think inkjet printers. Buying the printer itself is relatively inexpensive, less than $100 in some cases (and far less than it cost to make the printer), but to use it, you have to repeatedly buy printer ink cartridges at a relatively high price (a price that far exceeds what it costs the company to manufacture it.)

Investors become fond of certain business models, mostly because of past successes, but the most influential aspect of your business model is that you have one. Meaning, you are deep enough into the interaction with your customers that a clear and agreeable model exists for delivering value (your product or service) to your customer, and at a price and billing frequency that keeps the customer happy. Investor-ready startups have interacted with their customers enough to confidently describe the startup's business model.

Marketing and Marketing Calendar

Marketing efforts aim to create awareness of your product. Depending on your product and how you reach your customers, you might need to market to several types of people: end users, distribution channel partners, retailers, and so on. One of the more powerful tools in your investor-ready kit is a marketing calendar.

The marketing calendar document details your key marketing events and activities across a calendar or timeline layout. The calendar lays out development tasks, product launches, early customer feedback milestones, tradeshow dates, and social media campaigns plans, with associated time estimates attached. Log an estimated budget with each marketing activity on the calendar.

A detailed marketing calendar enables you to derive your guesses about the number of customers reached by the marketing efforts. You can then use those guesses as a foundation for your sales forecasting.

Sales Process and Sales Pipeline

Your marketing activities create awareness of your product, and then it's up to your sales team (or processes) to convert those who are now aware into paying customers.

As with marketing, you might be selling to several types of customers, depending on the nature of your product and the channels to your customers. A Business to Business (B2B) sales effort usually involves convincing several players within the prospect business: the end user of the product, a technical buyer (IT department, for example), an economic buyer (purchasing department), and perhaps a political buyer (CEO or CFO). B2B sales cycles can be long due to the number of players involved.

A Business to Consumer (B2C) sales model, such as a Internet retailer, or SaaS website, can be a more direct, with customer choosing to buy your product within a few minutes of visiting your site.

No matter what your sales model is, you need to be able to show the moving parts to investors. A sales process diagram and a sales pipeline log, are two tools you can use to show investors you have stabilized your sales model, and know how to convert prospects into paying customers.

- **Sales Process Diagram.** This one-page document shows the overall mechanism you use to get and convert customers or sign up users. Your sales process diagram should also show how many prospects you need at each stage to meet the sales revenue goals you've set for a given period. The following steps show an example B2B sales process:

  1. Warm Intro Email. This email would explain who referred you to the person you're writing, include a quick overview of our product, and specify that you would like the opportunity to talk.

  2. Follow-up Call. After a positive response to the warm intro email, seek to get an in-person meeting to answer questions.

  3. In-person Meeting. Next, schedule a meeting to present benefits of our solution, demo the product.

  4. Pilot Order. Ask the customer to place a limited pilot order, which gets the customer using the product, subsequently giving you the opportunity to solicit feedback and understand objections.

  5. Long-term contract. Negotiate and sign a contract, and engage your startup's customer service team for ongoing orders and support.

- **Sales Pipeline Log.** This is a working document (usually an Excel workbook) used to manage your sales effort. The pipeline log documents your sales prospects, key player names and contact information, which products those customers are interested in, how much (in units or revenue) they are likely to buy, your estimated chance of closing the client, and the resulting revenues. Also track other factors, such as next steps that need to happen with the client, and key objections to overcome. There are also many online tools used to manage the sales process, with SalesForce.com being one of the most popular.

- **Online Sales Models.** For Internet, mobile app and other online sales models, you need to track other factors, such as page visits, unique visitors, click through rates, and conversion rates. Illuminating these processes for investors helps remove doubt from the conversation.

Financial Projections

Your financial model ties together all the assumptions you've made about your startup. Investors know financial projections are educated guesses at best, but they want to know you have carefully thought through all the details of getting sales, setting pricing, managing costs, and determining how much you will need to spend each month to keep the startup alive and growing.

 Creating Financial Projections is Laughable

Many Internet and software entrepreneurs, investors, and Silicon Valley startup gurus say that it's is ludicrous and laughable for founders to attempt to create financial projections. After all, how can a startup that is only a few months old know what the future will bring? They say that savvy investors should be able to connect the dots and follow the vision of the founders for the market opportunity. While there may some truth to these statements for an Internet startup testing its latest idea, other startups in more established markets can clearly benefit from building simple financial models and projections that show their assumptions about customers, sales revenues, costs, expenses, and profits or losses.

Avoid Top-Down Projections

It's tempting (and common) for entrepreneurs to use top-down approaches to create their sales projections. Statements such as "we expect to capture 1% of this 700 billion dollar market in 3 years, therefore our revenues will be 1.4 billion" seem to distill the opportunity into a conservative number. Unfortunately, top down approaches for revenue projections fall flat for investors. Top-down projections assume everything will work perfectly, but investors know that the opposite is true—startups need to overcome many setbacks, obstacles, and challenges. Top-down estimates lack detail about specific customers segments, leave out how much effort/cost is needed to reach the customers, don't reveal sales cycle durations, and so on. A better and more convincing approach to revenue projections is the "From the Ground Up" method.

From the Ground Up Financial Projections

Building your revenue projections using a ground-up model creates a much more believable build up to revenues in the eyes of most investors. The general approach to a ground-up forecast includes the following tasks, using Excel or another spreadsheet program to build the model and do the math:

- **Customers.** Make estimates of the number of new customers acquired each month, as well as the level of anticipated reorders from existing customers.

- **Typical Sale.** Define a "typical sale" for each customer in dollars and units, if applicable.

- Revenue. Multiply your customers by the typical sale for a revenue total each month.

- **Costs.** Next, detail your cost estimates to deliver your product/service (see "Cost of Goods Sold" in the glossary).

- **Gross Margin.** Subtract your product costs from the revenue totals to yield the gross margin.

- **Sales and Marketing Expense.** Detail your sales and marketing costs to reach and convince customers.

- **Operating Expenses.** Outline operating expense outlays each month needed to keep the doors open.

- **Profit or Losses.** Finalize the profit (or loss) by subtracting your sales, marketing, and operating costs from the gross margin.

- **Profits Take Time.** Monthly losses are expected for many months, or perhaps years. Investors know it takes time to build a company.

Additionally, some investors might request two additional financial reports: a cash flow forecast and a balance sheet. While these documents are mostly meaningless for very early stage startups, they will become much more important as your startup grows.

Cash Flow Model

This spreadsheet shows how money flows into and out of your startup. If you are selling physical products and buy large amounts of inventory, your cash flow model should show when these purchases are expected and how much cash you need to spend. Investors scan you cash flow spreadsheets to see when you will run out of money—something most founders are also interested in.

Balance Sheet

For startups, in simple terms the balance sheet shows:

1. How much money you have now.

2. Who owes you money.

3. Who you owe money to.

Investors want to know if the startup has any large loans or other debts that might be a drain on the startups cash reserves. Other sections of the balance sheet show shareholders' equity and retained earnings, and for pre-revenue startups, these entries are nothing more than "on paper" entries to make things balance.

Funding Needs and Uses

Investor-ready startups have detailed a funding needs and uses document that shows how much money is being raised in the current round, and how the angel money will be put to work. Many founders break the funding needs and uses document into three sections, as follows:

- **Existing Investments and Achievements.** This starting portion of the funding timeline shows the achievements and milestones already reached using the founders' personal funds, friends and family money, or other early investor money. This brief "look back" helps show investors that the founders can execute their plans and put money to effective use.

- **Significant Milestones.** This is the meat of the funding needs and uses document, showing the major milestones planned for this funding round, how much cash each key category/task consumes, and the associated timing and dependencies. This section should show that when the company achieves these major milestones, the company will increase in value. Example milestones include software development phases/sprints completed, minimally viable product (MVP) product launches, winning major customer contracts, hitting user registration targets, and signing key partnership deals.

- **Future Funding Needs.** A funding roadmap can also reach further out into the future, beyond current milestones and funding levels. Making some estimates about how much more money you will need to grow your company helps angels put their investment into perspective. For example, do you anticipate needing to raise a large Series A round from VCs? If so, angel investors will get diluted, which may not be a bad thing if the company reaches its goals. Figure 11 illustrates how the **Use of Funds** diagram might be planned for two phases, with each phase tied to an Angel investment round.

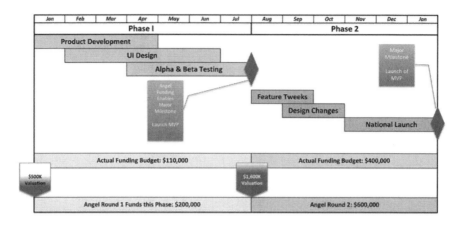

Figure 11. An example Use of Funds diagram, conveying major tasks and milestones in two phases.

Staying Alive: Burn Rate

"What is your burn rate?" is a common angel investor question. Investor-ready founders have given some thought to this question, both for their own planning, and to be ready to answer potential investors.

Burn rate for a startup is defined as how much money you spend each month to keep the startup alive. A typical burn rate figure accounts for costs such as:

- Direct costs associated with monthly sales, such as cost of goods sold, partner or affiliate fees, and so on.

- Estimated sales and marketing costs, including travel to customer sites, trade show fees, marketing costs, pay-per-click advertising fees.

- Salaries and wages to keep everybody showing up early and staying late.

86

- Other ongoing expenses such as rent, utilities, insurance, and Web hosting fees.

Additional items to note on your burn rate include:

- Are founders are deferring all or part of their salaries until cash flow supports it?

- Are there near term future events that will raise (or lower) your current burn rate, such as hiring a lead sales person?

Burn rates can range from lows of $2,000 to $5,000 per month for an early-stage startup to $50,000 to $150,000 or more per month for startups in later stages.

Investors always ask about the burn rate metric because they can use it to make a simple calculation that tells them how long your startup has to live, and how far any new investment will take you. Figure 12 illustrates an example calculation.

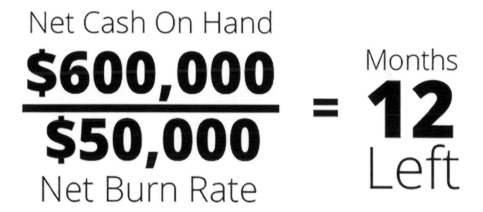

Figure 12. Investors use burn rate and this calculation to determine how long a startup can stay alive.

Market Size

How big is your defined market niche, both in dollars and number of customers? Creating a market size estimation shows investors you know who your potential customers are and have narrowed it down from "everybody" to a believable niche of highly passionate customers that will buy your product. There are two approaches to estimating the size of your potential market: from the ground up or from the top down.

Ground Up Market Size Estimation

1. **Define Your Ideal Customer.** Create a specific profile of your ideal customer, for example "acoustic guitarists who play Gibson and/or Fender guitars."

2. **Number of Ideal Customers.** Do research online and otherwise so you can estimate of the number of potential customers that meet your ideal customer profile. In a case like the example in the prior step, that number might be 500,000.

3. **Typical Sale.** Estimate a typical sale per customer. For example, you might find that the typical acoustic guitarist who favors Gibson and/or Fender spends $225 per purchase on products similar to yours.

4. **Do the Math.** Multiply the Number of Ideal Customers x Typical Sale = Total Market Size. Finishing out the above example, 500,000 Gibson/Fender customers x $225 typical sale = $112.5 million estimated market size.

Top Down Market Size Estimation

Using a top down approach to estimating market size is less desirable. A statement such as "We only need .02% of this $100 million market to hit our projections" characterizes this approach.

A top-down approach might indicate that you do can't strictly identify your ideal customer, so you've generalized and will attempt to figure it out later. Investors don't want to spend too much money for you stumble around for too long looking for customers. Do your homework, engage with customers very early in your startup, and show investors that customers will buy, then estimate how many of those ideal customers you can reach.

Market Growth

Another important factor related to the size of your potential market is its rate of growth (or decline). It goes without saying that investors like markets that are growing at a fast pace. Be prepared to illustrate the trends in your market segment, and be sure to be as specific as possible in terms of your identified market niche. For example, if your startup creates mobile gaming apps, be sure to pinpoint your target user, such as girls between the ages of eight and 15. Then back up your estimates with industry data that shows rapid growth of smartphone adoption by this same age group.

Competition

Investors (and everybody else) will always ask "Who else is doing what you are doing?" Be ready for this question by developing a one-page competitive summary. This summary should detail some of the factors described next.

Key Competitor Comparison

This simple chart or diagram in the competitive summary shows investors who your number one competitor is, as well as identifying other key competitors. If you can't compete with the number one competitor, the rest don't matter much. The chart compares product features or benefits and shows how your offering exceeds what the competition offers. It's important to be objective and build credibility when discussing your competitors. If a competitor's product has advantages over yours, point those out and explain why you will succeed in overcoming those advantages. Figure 13 shows an example competitive comparison chart.

	Our Startup	Key Competitor #1
Team	Deep App Technical & Industry Insiders	Legacy Technical & Industry Insiders
Software Approach	SaaS Model: Web App & Mobile	Desktop Software
Pricing	Low Monthly Fee	Upfront Fee + Monthly Maintenance
Market Partnerships	MOU with AARP	Pilot with SBA

Figure 13. An example competitive comparison chart emphasizes a major advantage—a SaaS business model.

One Big Advantage

It is better to have one big competitive advantage than several small ones and to detail that key advantage in the competitive summary. Adding up several small advantages might seem to show that you can get ahead, but in reality it's easy for your competitor to add small features or functionality or new marketing twists, and so on. Competing against one large advantage presents a more difficult barrier for your competition and would likely require major shifts in a competitor's course. Also, investors can remember one large advantage more easily.

Also, It's not just about better product features. More importantly, do you have a better way to reach your customer niche, or a better way to interact with your customers? For example, all of your competitors offer their product as installable desktop software, you are the first to provide it as a SaaS model, and you are 1.5 years ahead of any body else. Investors will respond to competitive advantages that are hard to duplicate.

Potential Entrants

This information in the competitive summary shows players in the market that might take notice of your traction and enter the market with their own product. Potential entrants are often larger established companies that have large budgets and resources. One of the frequent questions asked by investors is "What if the 800-pound gorilla (think Google for example) copies your product?" The best answer to this sort of challenge is that your startup can out maneuver the bulkier company, engage with customers faster, and add paying customers quicker than even the sharpest in-house corporate staff, even Google's. Leave it up to the investor to decide if this is true or not, and move on. Keep in mind as well that potential entrants often also represent potential exit partners for your startup, choosing to buy your company rather than create their own version, so interest in your company from a larger player could mean good news down the line.

 Head in the Sand

Some founders prefer to ignore the competition and drive forward with their plans. Think twice if this is your impulse, because doing some research on your competitors is not just about creating justification for angel investors. Understanding who you're competing with is necessary due diligence for you and your co-founders. If you have a well funded and later stage competitor directly in your space, a few hours of strategy time might reveal if there is way you can capture a portion of the competitor's market share.

Key questions you and investors should be asking include:

- How far ahead of the competition are you, in time, man-hours of research or development, and other product metrics?

- How well funded is the competing team?

- Have the competition pivoted and changed their approach to customers?

- How experienced are the competing team members?

- What is your "unfair advantage" over these competitors?

Competitors Validate New Markets

The existence of competitors can help validate a new or emerging market segment. Investors get nervous if your startup goes solo after a new market. Details about a competitor's technology, product features, or market approach provide a good reference point to help validate your product offering. If you have a strong product advantage, comparing it to a known competitor's offering can validate your position in the market.

Patents and Other IP

If your startup rests on new technology or breakthrough processes, you will likely seek patents and other forms of intellectual property protection. The importance of patents for startups is widely debated, but some angels feel like patents provide their investment additional protection from competitors entering the market.

If you are developing patents and other IP like trademarks or copyrights, present the status of your IP in a concise manner, including specifics when you pitch to investors. Examples include:

- "We have filed a provisional patent, as of January 2013."

- "We have filed a full utility patent, as of this date."

- "Our patent application is being prosecuted now, and we have a first office action."

- "Our patent has been issued under number 8384895830 and assigned to the corporation."

In addition to being clear about the status of any IP your startup has created, investor-ready founders have kept their housekeeping up to date with the following IP related paperwork:

- **Work-for-Hire Agreements.** Trademarks, logo designs, packaging design, website design and navigation, and many other branding elements of your startup can be critical elements of success. Be sure to use simple "work for hire" agreements with any designers or contractors that you hire for design and creative work. Work for hire agreements will help ensure that any IP associated with the design work is property of the startup, and not the sub contractor's.

- **Invention Assignment Agreements.** Investors will want to know that any intellectual property that has been created is properly assigned to the startup legal entity. As part of the early steps in forming a startup, founders usually sign Founders Stock Purchase Agreements that assign all IP rights they may have already created or acquired (code written or domain names purchased by a founder) to the corporation in exchange for their shares of founders' stock. Additionally, founders and early employees typically sign Invention Assignment Agreements that spell out the IP ownership for any new IP created going forward.

Valuation

Investor-ready founders understand the key role your valuation plays in the fundraising process. Building a valuation model for your startup *before* talking with angel investors prepares you for this discussion with investors. As discussed earlier, your pre-money valuation is the key component used to determine how much equity an investor gets for his/her money.

There are several methods for arriving at a pre-money valuation for your startup. See section "Valuation Methods" for more details about arriving at a valuation. Creating a one-page valuation spreadsheet showing how you arrived at your pre-money valuation shows investors you understand the process of raising money.

Is Your Startup Housekeeping Done?

You need to complete several housekeeping tasks (or at least get them underway) prior to seeking an angel funding round. The following list is a good starting point for these tasks:

- **Incorporate.** Establish your legal corporate entity either as an LLC, S corporation, or C corporation, and register for a federal tax ID, also known as an EIN (Employer Identification Number).

- **Find Legal Representation.** Establish a relationship with a lawyer experienced in startups. Startups involve specific legal issues you need to navigate with the help of a legal expert. Paying your hometown general practice lawyer to "learn as he goes" and try to understand the details of an investment term sheet will not serve your startup well.

- **Find CFO and Accounting Services.** Establish fee-based part time relationships with a CFO consultant and accountant. Getting expert financial and tax advice at the early stages will keep you out of trouble when things get really busy.

- **Set Up Banking.** Open a business bank account for the startup. You'll need the ability to make electronic payments, write checks, and have a place to put all the money you'll be making. Once you have formed your startup corporation, be sure not to co-mingle personal money with startup money. Keep everything separated and get a credit card for the business as well.

- **Create In-House Accounting Systems.** Get some basic accounting software in place, and pay a professional CPA to help establish your chart of accounts and help build a process for issuing purchase orders, invoicing clients, and receiving payments. Make sure you have designated an in-house person to handle these financial transactions, because if your startup handles these functions piecemeal between multiple players, items can begin to fall through the cracks. You can't make product if you can't order materials, and you can't get paid if you don't issue invoices.

7

Building Your Startup Funding Knowledge Base

Now that you've learned more about the angel funding process and what it takes to get investor ready, let's take a deeper look at some of the topics touched on earlier. You don't need to become an expert in all of these areas. However, you do need to learn enough to avoid pitfalls that have tripped up other entrepreneurs.

Understanding Startup Funding Speak

Spend enough time around startup investors and other founders and you are likely to hear a number of terms thrown around, like tranche and round. The following list helps define some of the most common startup fund raising terms:

- **Round (Investment Round).** The process and result of raising money for your startup is called a *round* or a *raise*. Whether you are at the beginning stages of the money raising process, or have just put an investors money in the bank, each round is given a name or designation, such as Seed round or Series A round.

  A round is also usually further defined by the amount of money being raised, as in "We are completing a seed round of $200,000". Or, "a west coast VC came in to complete our 2.5 million Series A round."

- **Friends and Family Round.** Money raised from friends and family—people you know well and are motivated to see you succeed in your new venture. Friends and family investments can take many forms, such as simple loans, gifts, or more complex equity investments that transfer shares in the startup to the friends and family investors. F&F rounds can be any size, but are usually small in size compared to angel rounds. as little as a few thousand dollars to more than $50,000 "pay when you can" loan from dad or a rich uncle. There are many nuances and cautions associated with taking money from friends and family, so be sure it's money they can afford to lose, and put the arrangement in writing so all expectations are crystal clear.

- **Seed Round.** In common usage, a seed round can be any investment in a startup used to start the company and create its first products or services. Money coming from the founders themselves, friends and family, or other support associated with the entrepreneurs that are starting the company can all qualify as a seed round. In contrast, the high-tech Silicon Valley definition of seed round is a bit different. Many large venture capital firms (VCs) have established seed funds with the purpose of backing very early innovations (almost to the point of experiments) that can disrupt very large industries. The amounts invested in seed rounds by these VCs are sometimes large ($1, $2, or even $3 million), as compared to angel funding rounds in the sub $1 million range.

- **Series A, Series B, etc.** Series A is a term used to mean many things, but typically, a Series A is the first VC level investment round. Additional investments from institutional investors follow the same pattern, Series B, Series C, and so on. Recall that VCs are in the business of investing other institutions money, not personal money from angels or friends and family investors.

In reality, the naming of your funding rounds can be anything thing you want to define—there are no set rules. For example, the popular Y-Combinator technology startup accelerator calls their investment rounds Series AA.

- **Tranche.** Rhyming with "carte blanche", a tranche is a disbursement of investment or loan dollars to a startup in stages. For example, "The investment will be disbursed to the startup in two tranches of $75,000 and $125,000, tied to specific milestones." In this example, investors have agreed to provide startup capital with a total amount of $200,000, but the funds are given to the startup in stages, attached to specific milestones. Milestones might include completing a prototype, signing a customer deal, or hitting a sales revenue target. Of the $200,000, the first tranche might be $75,000 to complete the prototype of the mobile app, and the next $125,000 tranche might be issued to launch a targeted marketing campaign. (for those who care, tranche is a French word meaning a slice or cutting.)

Equity and Debt Basics

There are two ways startups raise cash: selling equity or taking on debt. Equity aligns everyone's interest in the startup and preserves cash. Equity investments do not require monthly debt repayment, with the rare exception of dividend stipulations in some deals.

Equity is the ownership of the company, or who owns how much. Here are the key things you need to know about startup equity with regard to angel investments:

- At the formation stage of a startup, the founders decide on a fair equity split of the company shares. This can be a complicated process to get right, but many founders simplify the decision by splitting the ownership stake equally, for example, with three founders 33.3% is owned by each. Two founders might split ownership at 50% each. If there is only one founder of the company, he/she owns 100% to start.

- As the startup sells shares of company stock for cash from investors, they are selling a portion of the ownership of the company.

- When your startup sells shares, you are also giving up some level of control in the company, but at the angel level of investment, this is usually not much as long as the founders retain a majority stake in the corporation.

- The upside for investors is that their equity ownership enables them to share in the proceeds if the startup has a liquidity or exit event—that is, gets acquired by a larger company.

- There is generally no cash repayment to the investors, at least not on a monthly basis.

- Founders are charged with using the invested cash to increase the value of the startup, bring their product to market, and build a viable company.

- Investors hope the startup grows revenues and profits and ultimately gets acquired (exits) by a larger company.

- If the startup exits, the investors are likely to get a return on their money.

- Investors also share a great deal of risk in the startup. There is no guarantee that the startup will survive, let alone have an exit. And even if there is an exit, there is no guarantee that the deal would offer a large enough multiple (of revenue or profit) to represent the high return the founders and investors had hoped for.

- Founders dilute their percentage ownership in the startup, but the money from investors enables founders to grow the valuation of the company, making the pie bigger for founders and investors.

In contrast to equity funding, here are the key points to understand if your startup is considering taking on debt:

- The startup gets a loan from a bank or other lending institution.

- The loan is repaid on a monthly basis, principal and interest.

- The loan payback affects the cash outlay of the startup each month.

- The startup pays principal and interest on the loan to the lender, but the lender does not share in the upside if the company does well.

- Lenders have limited downside. If the startup fails, debt holders like banks are first in line to be repaid (if there are any assets left).

- It is very uncommon for banks to loan money to startups. The startup does not have a financial history or cash flow that points to the ability to repay a loan.

- Founders can tap a Home Equity Line of Credit (HELOC) secured by their personal real estate assets (personal home), but keep in mind this adds to the personal risk of funding your startup.

Dilution and Ownership Math

It is important for founders to have a clear understanding how much of the startup founders and investors own and the effects of taking on angel investors in terms of giving up a portion of that ownership. Share price is a measure of the (hopefully) increasing value of the company. When it comes to understanding ownership in the startup, the number of shares and share prices do not matter. Instead, the percentage of shares owned by each party represents the relative part of the company owned.

Dilution occurs when existing shareholder ownership percentages decreases as new investors come aboard. Dilution is a natural part of the process and not a bad thing. As long as the valuation of the startup is growing, dilution is not so bad for founders. You may own a smaller percentage of the startup, but the overall pie is getting bigger, so the value of your shares is larger too. Dilution of founders stock is expected because you are trading some ownership for much needed cash to grow your startup.

You should know these basics about the ownership math for your startup:

- **Total Shares Issued.** The cap table of the startup should log how many shares have been issued to stakeholders.

- **Shares You Own.** Keep clear records on how many shares you own in the startup.

- **Ignore Authorized Shares.** The number of authorized shares is established when the startup is formed, to create a general pool of shares to issue to stakeholders. The number of Authorized shares is a somewhat arbitrary number and does not influence your percentage ownership in the company.

- **Little Number Divided by Big Number.** To determine your percentage ownership for your startup, divide the number of shares you own by total shares issued.

For a more detailed look at ownership math, see "Understanding Fully Diluted Shares Outstanding," next.

Understanding Fully Diluted Shares Outstanding

When you consider ownership percentages, you need to make sure to use a fully diluted number for total shares outstanding. "Fully diluted" means that the total shares issued accounts for the number of shares issued or "spoken for." (Authorized but unissued shares of stock in your startup are not counted in the fully-diluted capitalization number.)

To be fully diluted, the total shares issued number typically includes:

- All outstanding common stock
- All outstanding preferred stock (on a converted to common basis)
- Outstanding warrants

- Outstanding options
- Options reserved for future grant
- Any other convertible securities on an "as converted" to common basis

Take a simplified example. Let's say you've calculated that there are 10 million fully diluted shares outstanding for your startup. As a founder, you own two million shares. If you divided your shares by the fully diluted shares as illustrated in the formula in Figure 14, you would get a result of .2 or 20%. With your 20% ownership, if the company were to sell for $10 million, you would get $2 million of that (assuming no preferred shares have participation rights or other preferences over your common shares rights, topics covered next).

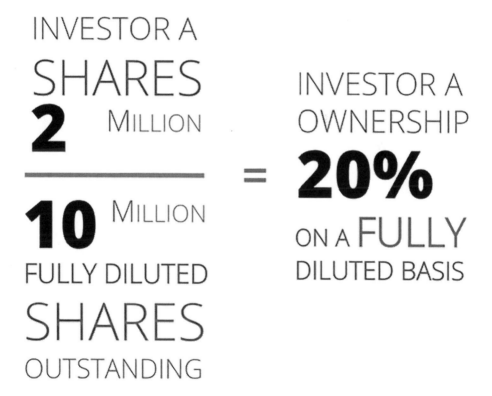

INVESTOR A
SHARES
2 MILLION

―――――――― **=**

10 MILLION
FULLY DILUTED
SHARES
OUTSTANDING

INVESTOR A
OWNERSHIP
20%
ON A FULLY
DILUTED BASIS

Figure 14. The formula for calculating ownership percentage.

Preferred Shares versus Common Shares

As touched on above, in return for an equity stake in your startup, you could issue a number of different types of securities. The two most basic "flavors" of securities are types of stock—preferred stock and common stock. Prior to any outside investment in the startup, only common shares exist. Founders and possibly employees own these common shares. When outside investors enter the equation, preferred shares are created as part of the investment process for the round. The term sheet outlines specific investor preferences, and details set in the stock purchase agreement and the restated or amended certificate of incorporation. As a startup founder, you need to understand the differences between the two types of shares and how they affect outcomes in your company.

Preferred shares

Angel investors often request preferred shares when they invest in a startup. "Preferred" means that they get certain rights with their shares. These rights provide the preferred shareholder protections, such as getting paid back first before common stock shareholders.

Rights included with preferred shares might include:

- **Participation Preference.** In the event of an exit, preferred holders "participates" with the common shareholders to split up the proceeds of the acquisition, after any liquidation preferences have been fulfilled.

- **Liquidation Preference.** If there is an exit, the investor gets a disbursement of money equal to the invested amount, or a multiple of the original investment, referred to as a 1X (one times), 2X (two times), and so on, liquidation preference. This right is often combined with the participation preference. Most investors do not want to gouge founders, so this point is negotiable.

- **Anti-Dilution Preference.** Versions of this preference protect the investor against a down-round, where the current investment round is being executed at a lower valuation than the previous investment round. You and your investors always want your startup valuation to increase. When the pie is getting smaller, investors seek to maintain their current percentage ownership using anti-dilution preferences.

- **Voting Rights.** As a standard practice, only common shareholders vote on key issues of the startup, but over time, angel investors seek to protect and influence the outcome of their investment. Getting voting rights on major issues in a startup is one way angel investors exert this influence. Preferred shares voting right clauses include specifics, such as having the right to vote with common shareholders on issues such as:

    o Changes to the articles of incorporation

    o Changes to the corporate bylaws

    o Changes to the size of the board of directors

    o Employee salary levels (including founder salaries)

    o Raising additional capital or debt

    o Liquidation or dissolution of the corporation

Common Shares

Founders and employees typically hold common stock. When founders form the corporate entity, they decide what percentage of the company each founder owns. Later, when they decide to seek outside investment and perform other corporate housekeeping, they determine how to divide ownership percentages into stock shares and issue themselves common shares. Common shares have no special rights or leverage. They are the most basic representation of ownership in the company.

The number of common shares you own on a fully diluted basis represents your percentage ownership in the company, as detailed earlier.

Common shares typically afford you voting rights on key decisions in the startup, although startups can create non-voting common shares. Your percentage ownership determines the weight of your vote. If you own 55% of the common shares, your vote has a weight of 55% relative to the other voters.

Common share owners are typically last in line to get paid in the event of an exit or dissolution of the company. Debt holders such as banks or other lenders are first in line, followed by any preferred shareholders, and then common stock holders are last— so negotiate preferred share rights carefully.

Convertible Debt

It is not uncommon for angels to make early investments in startup in the form of convertible debt, also referred to as a convertible note. In a convertible debt investment deal, the investor makes a loan to the company (the debt), and that loan converts into equity at some point in the future, with an extra bonus to the investor for taking on higher risk of the early-stage startup. If you're not familiar with how convertible debt works, here are the basics:

- **Delayed Valuation.** Convertible debt provides a method to raise money without putting a valuation on the company at the time when you issue the debt. For early stage startups, it is difficult to put a valuation on the company. Not enough progress has been made toward bringing your product to market, so the longer you can delay setting a valuation, the more leverage you will have to raise money later.

- **Interest Rate Earned.** The holder of the convertible note (the angel), earns interest on the note, just like a bank loan with an interest rate. The startup does not actually make payments on the loan, or the interest. The interest accrues over the term of the note and gets added into the total value of the note when it converts to the new class of shares that are negotiated in the next valued round.

- **Conversion Trigger.** Typically, the convertible notes "converts" at a defined "trigger event", most often when the startup raises its first valued round, meaning you and the next round of investors agree on a pre-money valuation of the startup. The convertible note is then converted into X number of preferred shares, with the same rights and price as established in the negotiations with the valued round investors.

- **Discount Rate Sweetener.** Convertible notes also carry a discount rate that sweetens the deal for the note holder. The note holder gets to buy the newly valued stock as a discount from the stock price associated with the valuation established with the new investors, thus getting more shares for their money. Discounts range between 15% to 25%.

- **Low Legal Fees.** Fewer legal documents are required to execute a convertible note agreement, and the startup typically pays the legal fees associated with fund raising.

- **Speed.** Convertible debt can be a faster way to get an investment deal done. Because a valuation does not need to be established or negotiated, convertible notes are often a faster way for founders to raise money.

Restricted Stock

As covered earlier, when the startup is formalized (incorporated as an LLC, S corporation, or C corporation), the founders determine what equity percentage each founder owns and subsequently issue stock shares reflecting those percentages. Stock shares are then issued to the founders. Many startups choose to structure the founder shares as restricted stock, using a restricted stock purchase agreement (RSPA)

Under an RSPA, some or all of each founder's shares are reserved or "taken away," and "earned" back over time. The longer the founder is into the vesting schedule, the more shares have been earned back. The restricted shares are assigned to the corporation, so no other person owns them. If you leave the startup before your restricted shares vest, the shares can be used by the corporation to recruit other talent.

Restricted stock offers a number of benefits, such as:

- Instills commitment among founders: "We're all in this together."
- Provides investors some level of assurance that founders have an incentive to follow through.
- Helps prevent a critical team member from leaving.

A common vesting schedule is **four years, with a one year cliff for the first 25%, and then each additional 1/48th of the shares are earned each month thereafter.** The "cliff" terminology means that the shareholder has to wait the duration of the cliff period, a full year (in this example) before he/she earns any shares. Thus providing a hefty incentive for the founder to get things done and stay the course. Figure 15 shows a graphical example of a vesting schedule.

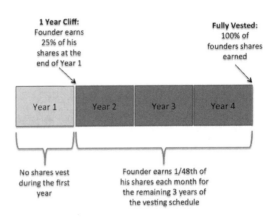

Figure 15. A four year vesting schedule with a one year cliff.

Cap Tables

A cap (capitalization) table is a document (usually an Excel spreadsheet) that tracks **who owns how much of a company**. For each investment round, the cap table spells out these details:

- **Investment Amount, Share Types and Ownership.** The table lists the number and type of shares owned by the founders, by investors, by employees, and any other stakeholders in the company.

- **Option Pools.** Stock option pools are listed, and the impact of exercised options is often included in the calculations.

- **Valuation and Share Prices.** Pre-money valuation is listed and a post-money valuation is calculated. The sheet also calculates share price based on these inputs: the valuation, investment amount, option pool shares, and the total shares outstanding.

- **What-If Tool.** A cap table enables the entrepreneur and investor to see the effect of their negotiations. It includes what-if calculations based on the amount invested, shows how much founders get diluted, and shows the resulting percentage ownership of all shareholders. Founders and investors can plug in different investment amounts and valuations into the cap table, and see how the resulting percentages compare.

- **Exit Scenarios.** More elaborate cap tables enable exit scenarios to be calculated, calculating how much founders, investors, and options holders make if the company gets acquired at various acquisition prices.

Figure 16 shows an example startup cap table.

Shareholders	Stock Type	Startup Formation Founders' Shares	Fully-Diluted Stock %	First Angel Round Shares This Round	Total Post-Round Shares	Fully-Diluted Stock %	Second Angel Round Shares This Round	Total Post-Round Shares	Fully-Diluted Stock %
Startup Formation									
Founder A	Common	1,000,000	40.0%		1,000,000	33.3%		1,000,000	26.7%
Founder B	Common	1,000,000	40.0%		1,000,000	33.3%		1,000,000	26.7%
First Angel Round									
Independent Angel	Common			500,000	500,000	16.7%		500,000	13.3%
Second Angel Round									
Angel Group	Preferred						750,000	750,000	20.0%
First VC Round									
VC #1	Preferred								
Pre-Money Options									
Option Pool	Common	500,000	20.0%		500,000	16.7%		500,000	13%
Totals		2,500,000	100%		3,000,000	100%		3,750,000	100%

Startup Formation — Pre-Money Valuation: N/A; Investment Amount: None; Post-Money Valuation: N/A; Shares Outstanding: None; Price Per Share: $0.001

First Angel Round — Pre-Money Valuation: $1,000,000; Investment Amount: $200,000; Post-Money Valuation: $1,200,000; Shares Outstanding: 2,500,000; Price Per Share: $0.40

Second Angel Round — Pre-Money Valuation: $2,000,000; Investment Amount: $500,000; Post-Money Valuation: $2,500,000; Shares Outstanding: 3,000,000; Price Per Share: $0.67

Figure 16: An example cap table.

Term Sheets

If angels are interested in investing in your startup, they will begin discussing the general terms of an investment in your startup, including how large an investment to make, what percentages of equity will result for the investors, valuation, board structure and seats, and so on. As covered earlier, a written document called the term sheet outlines these factors, as well as other "protections" the investors would like to establish.

Most notably, many angels want a new preferred class of stock to be created that helps protect their investment. As discussed earlier in the book, preferred shares get additional rights or "preferences" tied to them, adding to the protections the angels get, such as getting paid back first in line in the event of an exit. The term sheet outlines these preferences.

Typical term sheet sections include:

- Pre-money valuation of the startup

- The amount of the investment to be made

- Post-money valuation

- Type of security, typically preferred stock, and numbers of shares

- Dividend

- Option pool size

- Warrants and conversion terms

- Anti-dilution preferences

- Legal fees and who pays them

- Co-sale or right of first refusal: If the founder sells his or her stake, so can the investor, at the same terms.

- Board seats: The investor gets the designate a board of director member, usually one of the angels.

- Voting rights

- Information rights

 Not a Contract

A term sheet is not a contract or a promise to invest, but rather an agreement in principle that outlines the terms of the investment deal.

Early-stage Startup Valuation

How to think about startup valuation

To get started, let's review some of the basic ideas of early-stage startup valuation.

- At the very early stages of your startup the company has

very little value.

- As you accomplish milestones in your startup (build product, get customers) the value of your company increases.

- If you are working to raise money from investors (equity funding), founders trade a portion of their ownership for cash investment.

- The investment amount raised from investors and the valuation of your company determines how much equity ownership you give up to the investors.

- There are no exact formulas for determining early-stage valuations.

- The valuation of your company is established by agreement between you and the investor.

- Investors want a low valuation (before they put their money in).

- Founders want a high valuation.

Next, the percentage equity owned by investors after the funding round closes is expressed by this simple equation:

$$\frac{\text{Raise Amount } \$250{,}000}{\$1{,}250{,}000 \text{ Post-Money Valuation}} = \text{Investor } \mathbf{33\%} \text{ Ownership}$$

There are many ways to arrive at the pre-money valuation for a startup. All methods involve educated guesswork and are more art than science. Two common methods are the risk mitigation method and scorecard method.

Risk Mitigation Valuation Method

This method assigns dollar values to the accomplishments and validations of the startup in four categories of risk mitigation: Technology, Market, Execution (team), and Capital. The values are either actual dollars spent to achieve the task or estimations of the "worth" of the item/outcome. See the following example of what a ground-up valuation might look like.

Technology Risk Mitigation

- Prototype developed: $75,000
- 3rd party testing completed: $10,000
- IP underway: $15,000

Market Risk Mitigation

- Market research: $20,000
- Early Adopter Program in place: $25,000
- Channel partners established: $40,000

Execution Risk Mitigation

- Experienced founders, previous startups: $200,000
- Prior exit: $100,000
- Detailed execution roadmap in place: $10,000

Capital Risk Mitigation

- Early funding (friends and family): $35,000
- Only two Angel Rounds needed: $50,000

Add up all the values to get the risk mitigation valuation, $580,000 in this example.

One of the advantages of a risk mitigation valuation is that comprised of many smaller elements or small victories. An investor can argue that one number is too high, but since it's a small piece of the total valuation, the impact of lowering the line-item value impacts the total less.

Scorecard Valuation Method

The scorecard valuation method applies weights to several categories of "impact" and scores the startup better or worse against a "typical" startup in the industry. This valuation method is detailed on the Gust.com website. (Payne, 2011)

Figure 17 shows an example scorecard valuation model. Factors such as the strength of the startup team, the size of the opportunity (the long term revenue size of the startup), and the need for additional investment are given weights of importance, and the startup is scored for each category with a percentage that indicates if it is better or worst than a typical startup. The score and weight are multiplied and the result is a number that represents how the startup being scored fairs in that category. In the Figure 17 example, the strength of the entrepreneur and team category is given an importance weight of 30% (very important as compared to the other weights), and a score of 125%, meaning the startup is 25% better than the average. These two numbers are multiplied, resulting in a factor of .38. This is done for all of the comparison factors on the scorecard. All of the factors are added up to get a total multiplier of 1.18, meaning that this startup is viewed to be 18% more valuable than an average startup in this space. And, if the valuation for an average startup in this space is 1.5 million, then this startup is valued at 1.76 million (or 18% more than 1.5 million).

Comparison factor	Range	Startup Score	Factor
Strength of Entreprenuer and team	30%	125%	0.38
Size of Opportunity	25%	125%	0.31
Product/Technology	15%	125%	0.19
Competitive Environment	10%	100%	0.10
Marketing/Sales/Partnerships	10%	125%	0.13
Need for additional Investment	5%	75%	0.04
Other factors	5%	75%	0.04
		Total	1.18
Standard Startup Valuatiuon in this Segment (millions)			$1.5
		Pre-Money Value (millions)	$ 1.76

Figure 17. An example score card pre-money valuation calculation.

Say No… To an Accounting Valuation

Accountants have a very different view of company valuation. They are trained to use discounted cash flow and other accounting methods of calculating a company's valuation. These methods are well tested for established companies that have several years of financial actuals to review, but are of no use what so ever for valuing early stage startups.

Founders should use several methods to make their estimates for the pre-money valuation of their startups, as well as find similar startups in their space and learn what valuations investors accepted for the funding rounds completed. Cruchbase.com is an excellent resource for researching startup valuations, sizes of angel and VC funding rounds, and much more startup data and statistics.

Legal Documents Pertaining to Angel Funding

There are a number of core legal documents that need to be updated or created to finalize an equity investment in a startup. Having a basic understanding of these documents is important for startup founders. This information is not intended to be legal advice of course—be sure to get a good startup lawyer to help you navigate the legal intricacies of taking on equity partners and completing the necessary paperwork. Inconsistencies and missing pieces missed at this stage can derail an investment closing.

The legal agreements typically associated with an equity investment include:

- **Stock Purchase Agreement.** The stock purchase agreement details the purchase of the startup's stock, the type of shares being granted to the investors (preferred typically), the number of shares, and share price.

- **Investors' Rights Agreement.** This document details the agreed upon rights that protect the angel investors. Typical rights include the right of first refusal, which enables the angel to maintain their proportional share (pro rata) ownership in the startup in the event of a future stock offering, meaning they are first in line to be offered any additional stock in the company. Additional rights include access to the startup's financial information and restrictions of transfer of stock.

- **Amended and Restated Certificate of Incorporation.** The certificate of incorporation (also called Articles of Incorporation) creates the new class of preferred stock for the angel transaction. The number of preferred shares authorized is defined and named, "Series AA Preferred Stock," for example, and the par value of the shares (usually a tiny amount such as .001/share) is set. Any specific rights tied to the preferred stock (negotiated in the term sheet)— liquidation preferences, conversion rights, voting rights, and so on—are also defined in this document. Along with the creation of the preferred class of shares, a matching number of additional common shares are authorized, in the event that the investors elect to convert their preferred shares to common.

- **Board Consent and Shareholders Consent.** These documents detail that the board of directors and current majority stockholders (usually the founders and any initial investors) consent to making the necessary changes to existing corporate legal documents so that the investor transaction can proceed. By executing these documents, the board members and founders agree to amending and restating the certificate of incorporation, agree to the creation of the new stock class, authorizes the corporate officers of the startup to execute the new agreements needed, and authorize the stock purchase agreement and investors' rights agreement.

Advisors and Board of Directors

A formal board of directors (BOD) of a company is the top governing body for the corporate entity. The executive management of the startup, the CEO, reports to the BOD. The BOD acts on behalf of the corporate entity, which includes shareholders, founders, and other stakeholders. A good startup BOD makes the founding team stronger, providing guidance, connections, and advice to help grow the company.

Do you need a formal board of directors before pitching to angels? No, but it's a good idea to form an advisory board to show you are willing to get input from experienced supporters. Many startups create their formal board of directors when they close their first angel investment round, in part because most angels/groups want a board seat as part of the terms of an investment in your business.

Some startups offer non-investor board members a small amount of equity as compensation. For example, a well recognized/ named strategic board member can help validate the mission of a startup to outside investors and target large customers. A very small percentage of equity (.5% to 1%, usually in the form of stock options) is well worth having a heavy hitter board member.

 Build It Fast and First

As a startup entrepreneur, your number one priority in building a startup is to get your product in the hands of potential customers. Get as far as you can without formal advisors or a board of directors, as they can slow you down. Too many meetings, status update requests, and unwanted opinions will drain your time. Use every scrap of your time to build and ship your product, then you can spend time working on the necessary fundraising and other house keeping for the corporation.

Once your startup has graduated to the level of needing angel investment and a formal board of directors, board members can contribute to building the startup in several ways:

- Fill gaps in skill sets of founders. For example, many founders lack financial expertise and a CFO skilled board member could provide insight and guidance to the correct financial methods or perspectives.

- Help during crisis, such as losing a co-founder to another startup, or losing a key customer.

- Set expectations, such as holding to product launch dates, or maintaining focus on building agreed upon sales channels.

- Provide a sounding board for new strategies, and review progress

- Be a source of appeal for management issues or conflicts between founders

- Keep the startup focused on strategic goals

When considering whether you need an advisory board or formal board of directors, keep the differences and matters of timing described next in mind.

Advisory Board

- You would typically form an advisory board during early stages of the startup.

- Advisory board member roles are non-voting, providing advice and guidance, not governance.

- Advisory board members have very limited or no liability with regards to activities related to your company.

- Due to the scope of their role, advisory board members are usually not compensated.

- Advisory board members are often strategic. Scientific experts, industry insiders, notable names all lend credibility to the startup's progress.

Formal Board of Directors (BOD)

- You typical form your BOD at investment close, as spelled out in the term sheet details.

- The BOD provides governance of the startup, with the CEO reporting to the BOD.

- The BOD carries a degree of legal liability, making Directors and Officers insurance sometimes necessary.

- Some non-investor BOD members receive some small amounts of equity compensation

- The BOD's loyalty is to the corporation, not founders or shareholders.

D&O Insurance

Formal BOD members have a legal obligation to the company they serve. They are potentially at risk in the event of a lawsuit. For this reason, most board members require the startup to take out an insurance policy to indemnify the board member from any legal problems that could arise from a lawsuit. This insurance is called Directors and Officers (D&O) insurance.

SEC Rules of Startup Funding

Even startup businesses are subject to Securities and Exchange Commission (SEC) rules covering company investments, including how much are you allowed to raise and what criteria transactions must meet. When raising angel funding in the form of equity, you are selling stock in your startup, and the SEC considers this selling a security.

The SEC says that securities must be *registered* with the SEC—a very expensive and time consuming process not in the achievable realm for a startup company. To solve this problem, the SEC made adjustments to their complex regulations so startups can raise money from investors and even inexperienced friends and family. These exemptions are known as Regulation D (Reg D) exemptions. Regulation D contains three rules or exemptions to the registration requirements: 504, 505, and 506. (You'll read more details about these shortly, and can read the official version here: http://www.sec.gov/answers/regd.htm)

There are four key questions to keep in mind when applying the rules:

- **Is the investor accredited?** As noted earlier in the book, an accredited investor has significant net worth or income. The SEC defines an accredited investor as having more than 1 million in net worth (not including primary residence) or more than $200,000 annual income (expected for the next two years) for an individual or $300,000 annual income for the household.

- **Is the investor sophisticated?** The purchaser of the stock has sufficient knowledge and experience in financials and business to understand the merits and risks of the investment.

- **Is the stock restricted?** The shares can not be resold to another party.

- **Is the stock being offered as a general solicitation or being advertised to the public?** General solicitation means the startup is offering or pitching the stock to people they do not know, similar to advertising to unknown potential investors.

Rule 504: The Seed Fund Exemption

Rule 504 allows you to raise up to $1 million within a 12 month period. The rule impacts your fundraising in these ways:

- **504 for Friends and Family.** Rule 504 is what most fund raising for startups falls under when they raise friends and family money. Friends and family usually do not meet the accredited investor criteria (although some do). If the investors are non-accredited and non-sophisticated, then they must be people you already know (meeting the no general solicitation criteria), AND the stock must be restricted from resale.

- **Rule 504 with Accredited Investors.** If the investors are accredited, like angels, then your can pitch audience can be strangers, and the stock does not need to be restricted. Pitching to a room full of angels you don't know is just fine, and is what happens every day all over the world.

Rule 505 Exemption

Under Rule 505 you can raise up to $5 million in a 12 month period. You can raise the money from a combination of:

- An unlimited number of accredited investors, and/or

- Up to 35 unaccredited investors

The stock must be restricted from resale and you may not use general solicitation or advertising to find your potential investors.

You must also provide prospective investors audited financial statements, as well as other disclosure documents that outline the risks of your startup in great detail.

Rule 506 Exemption

Rule 506 allows an unlimited amount of securities to be issued to:

- An unlimited number of accredited investors, and

- Up to 35 sophisticated non-accredited investors

Under this rule, several criteria must be met:

- The seller of the stock must be available to answer questions about the securities and company.

- Audited financial statements must be provided to prospective investors.

- The stock must be restricted from resale.

- No general solicitation or advertising may be done.

Jumpstart Waiver

A subpart (c) to rule 506 was added under the Obama Jumpstart Our Business Startups Act. Subpart 506 (c) allows for General Solicitation and Advertising, but the stock purchasers must be accredited. Also, much more diligence or proof of the accredited investor's net worth and income must be established by the startup, such as obtaining copies of tax returns, or references from certified professionals such as CPA or tax attorneys.

Additional Reg D Requirements

Founders raising angel funds under Reg D rules should also follow the SEC guidelines with the following tasks:

- **File Form D.** The startup needs to file a Form D with the SEC within 15 days after the first sale of the stock. This simple form includes the names and addresses of the executive officers of the startup and any stock promoters/advisors involved. The form must be filed online with detailed instructions found here:

  www.sec.gov/info/smallbus/secg/formdguide.htm

  Note that some states also require Form D to be filed with their securities regulation offices.

- **Consider Anti-Fraud.** Anti fraud rules apply for all sales of stock. Any information about the company, its prospects, or status must be free of any false or misleading information. Also, the information about the startup must not exclude any material information. If the omission creates a false or misleading understanding of the company or its prospects, it can be considered fraudulent.

- **Check State Law.** Founders should check with their state securities offices for any state-level regulations pertaining to small company stock offerings.

Thank You

This concludes the *Founder's Pocket Guide: Raising Angel Capital.* We hope you find our content and supporting tools useful for your startup journey.

We are always looking for feedback on our startup tools. If you have comments, feedback, or corrections, please send us a note.

info@1x1media.com

http://www.1x1media.com

End Notes:

Angel Capital Association website: www.angelcapitalassociation.org

AngelList public funding and detailed angel investment data: www.angel.co

The Angel Investor Market in 2012: A Moderating Recovery Continues (Sohl, 2013)

SEC Regulation D Details: http://www.sec.gov/answers/regd.htm

SEC Form D Filing: www.sec.gov/info/smallbus/secg/formdguide.htm

The Halo Report 2013 (The Angel Resource Institute, Silicon Valley Bank and CB Insights)

Valuations 101: Scorecard Valuation Methodology, Gust.com (Payne, 2011)

###

23367342R00070

Printed in Great Britain
by Amazon